THE
ROAD
TO SIENA

The Essential Biography of St. Catherine

St. Catherine of Siena, from an engraving

THE
ROAD
TO SIENA

The Essential Biography of St. Catherine

EDMUND G. GARDNER

EDITED WITH FOREWORD AND ANNOTATIONS BY
JON M. SWEENEY

PARACLETE PRESS
BREWSTER, MASSACHUSETTS

The Road to Siena: The Essential Biography of St. Catherine

2009 First Printing

Copyright © 2009 by Jon M. Sweeney

ISBN: 978-1-55725-621-8

Scripture quotations are taken from the *New Jerusalem Bible*, published and copyright ©1985 by Darton, Longman & Todd Ltd. and Doubleday, a division of Random House Inc., and are used by permission of the publishers.

Library of Congress Cataloging-in-Publication Data

Gardner, Edmund Garratt, 1869-1935.
  The road to Siena : the essential biography of St. Catherine / Edmund G. Gardner ; edited with foreword and annotations by Jon M. Sweeney.—[New ed.].
     p. cm.
  Rev. ed. of: Saint Catherine of Siena.
  Includes bibliographical references and index.
  ISBN 978-1-55725-621-8
  1. Catherine, of Siena, Saint, 1347-1380 I. Sweeney, Jon M., 1967- II. Gardner, Edmund Garratt, 1869-1935. Saint Catherine of Siena. III. Title.
  BX4700.C4G3 2009
  282.092—dc22
  [B]
                                                    2009012874
  10 9 8 7 6 5 4 3 2 1

Published by Paraclete Press
Brewster, Massachusetts
www.paracletepress.com
Printed in the United States of America

CONTENTS

FOREWORD

Edmund Garrett Gardner's classic work on St. Catherine of Siena was groundbreaking in its day, and it is still one of the most important biographies ever written of a medieval saint. It was originally published in 1907 under the title *Saint Catherine of Siena: A Study in the Religion, Literature and History of the Fourteenth Century in Italy*, by J. M. Dent & Co. in London, and E. P. Dutton & Co. in New York. In the bibliography published at the back of her own classic work *Mysticism: A Study in the Nature and Development of Spiritual Consciousness* (1911), Evelyn Underhill referred to Gardner's book with the following special, short sentence:

(The best modern biography.)

In fact, it was really the *only* modern biography of St. Catherine. But Underhill rarely made that sort of comment about the biographies of other saints; in conversation, she was known to advise people to read Gardner's *Saint Catherine of Siena* if they wanted to see how a biography of a saint *should* be written.

Edmund Gardner was the first to uncover and examine original documents related to the life of St. Catherine, left largely untouched for five centuries. Like any modern historian, he practiced textual criticism and historical criticism, and insisted on not simply retelling the legends of the saint for a new generation. As he explains in his Introduction, "I have been aided greatly by the manuscripts still preserved of Catherine's letters, manuscripts full of unpublished matter that has been unaccountably neglected, having apparently escaped the notice of all of her previous biographers and editors. This material throws light upon every aspect of the saint's genius and has enabled me, at many points, to correct erroneously accepted ideas about the events of her life and the order of her writings."

The original edition's advertisements, included by the publisher at the back of the 1907 book, included this intriguing sentence: "Much of the book is based upon hitherto unpublished documents in the Secret Archives of the Vatican, and in the libraries of Rome and Florence." The way that "Secret Archives" is capitalized might make you think that the publishers were attempting to be salacious, but it is true that Gardner was the first historian to uncover documents relating to Catherine's story, and there is indeed a room in the Vatican by that name! Today, the Vatican Secret Archives even has a website, and makes many texts available online.

But Gardner's were the days when Catholicism was still seen as somewhat suspect and a bit exotic and dangerous in England, where he lived and taught his university students. Even today, the 1701 Act of Settlement, which states that any royal descendent who is Catholic or married to a Catholic is "for ever" excluded from the line of succession, still stands. Members of the royal family still renounce their Catholic faith, or convert to the Church of England, in order to maintain their position. This happened as recently as May 2008, when the *Catholic News Agency* reported: "A woman engaged to a member of the British royal family has renounced her Catholic faith to maintain her fiancé's position in the line of succession. *The Times Online* reports that Autumn Kelly, 31, was received into the Church of England. She is to be married to Peter Phillips, Queen Elizabeth II's eldest grandson, on May 17."[1]

Edmund Gardner was a professor of Italian at Gonville and Caius College, Cambridge. He wrote many books over a long career, including books on Dante, English mystics, the city of Florence, the city of Siena, Arthurian legends, and Italian Renaissance painters. He also wrote many articles for the *Catholic Encyclopedia* (now easily accessed on the Web at newadvent.org), which was at the height of its groundbreaking compilation from 1907–14, the years of Gardner's most creative activity.

Throughout all of his books, Gardner was most fascinated by Christian mystics, and he tried to understand their unusual sort of knowledge and intuition. Nowhere is this seen more clearly than in Gardner's early work—a study of the third part of Dante's *Divine Comedy*, the *Paradiso*. He summarizes the theme of Dante's *Paradiso* thusly: "the mystical union of the soul with the First Cause in vision, love and enjoyment, and the comprehension of the most sublime and secret things of the celestial mysteries."[2]

One of Gardner's most reprinted essays, which first appeared in 1913 and is titled "The Science of Love," is also about the mysticism in Dante's *Paradiso*. Gardner begins in this way, by quoting Thomas Aquinas: "'Man,' writes Aquinas, 'has three kinds of knowledge of divine things. The first of these is according as man, by the natural light of reason, ascends through creatures into the knowledge of God; the second is in so far as the divine truth, exceeding human understanding, descends to us by way of revelation, not however as though demonstrated to our sight, but as set forth in words to be believed; the third is according as the human mind is elevated to the perfect intuition of the things that are revealed.'"[3] It was this third form of knowledge that most intrigued him.

It only remains—before turning to Gardner's remarkable recounting of the life of St. Catherine—to say a few words about the way in which Gardner's original work has been re-edited for the present edition. It was common a century ago for biographers to describe and display all of their tools before proceeding with the actual building of the building. The original preface to Gardner's masterwork does just this sort of thing, describing the dating of primary source materials, textual variances from one manuscript to another, and so on. I have removed most of this detail for two reasons. First, much of it has been superseded by subsequent scholarship over the century since it was first written. And second, because today's reader tends to have less interest in it; the reader who wants to delve into such subjects today will usually consult the scholarly journals that are read only by specialists.

Similarly, it was once the practice of biographers to leave most of the conclusions to the end. Today's reader of biography and history expects more of the information up front, and throughout. For this reason, I have re-edited what was Gardner's penultimate chapter on Catherine's literary legacy, and moved some of his conclusions to his Introduction, instead.

For those curious to compare, I have intentionally shortened Gardner's long narrative of the travels and many correspondents of Catherine, particularly between chapters 9 and 11. The title for chapter 10 is, in fact, my own, as I have combined some of what was in Gardner's original chapters 10 through 12. I have also rephrased many of Gardner's sentences, making the language more suitable for today's reader. In the process, some phrases have been deleted and others reworked. On occasion, a phrase or sentence has been deleted altogether, either because it is information that takes today's general reader into too much detail, or, because it tends to divert into the more sentimental sort of biographical writing—even in modern scholarship such as Gardner's. Most of the quotations from Scripture have been converted to the New Jerusalem Bible (NJB), used by permission; and quotations from *The Divine Comedy* by Dante Alighieri in the sidebar notes are from the famous Henry Wadsworth Longfellow translation.

The appendix to the original Gardner volume reproduced portions of six letters of St. Catherine, and two of them in total; and throughout Gardner's work (both in the original, and in this edition), he makes more use of Catherine's letters to tell her story than any other textual evidence. Gardner wrote in the original preface to his biography of his hope that a scholar in Italy would soon compile an authoritative, critical edition of the letters of St. Catherine in the original Italian. And then, as a footnote—the sort of footnote one might add when one's book is already in page proofs when a new and important piece of evidence comes to light—Gardner added: "An excellent selection from the letters, based on Gigli's [Italian] text, has been published in English by Miss Vida D. Scudder (London, 1905)." The Scudder edition, in fact, quickly became a spiritual classic in its own right. In what follows, I often quote from Scudder to further illuminate the ideas and progression of them in Gardner's account.

Despite its excellent reputation, as often happens, Gardner's great work on St. Catherine of Siena is hardly ever read today. We tend to value what's new much more than what is old, almost regardless of the quality of both. My own copy of Gardner's original work, with which I have labored to create this new edition, was borrowed from the rare book library of a nearby college. Sadly, but commonly, many of the book's pages, although more than a century old, had remained uncut (meaning also, unread) until the book passed into my hands. If you have never handled a book with uncut pages, this means that I had to literally use a knife to carefully remove the fore-edge of some of the pages in order to read them. This struck me as an apt symbol of why I work to create new editions of books such as Gardner's: my sincerest hope is that this new edition of Gardner's master-work of a master saint will bring a large, new audience to the study of Catherine of Siena.

[1] *Catholic News Agency*, May 2, 2008.
[2] Edmund G. Gardner, *Dante's Ten Heavens: A Study of the Paradiso* (New York: Haskell House Publishers, 1970), 1–2.
[3] Edmund G. Gardner, "The Science of Love," in *Dante and the Mystics* (New York: Haskell House Publishers, 1968), 298.

LIST OF ILLUSTRATIONS

St. Catherine of Siena, by Andrea di Vanni

THE
ROAD
TO SIENA

The Essential Biography of St. Catherine

INTRODUCTION

In this book I have not attempted to write the conventional biography of a canonized saint, but a study of Italian history centered in the work and personality of one of the most wonderful women that ever lived. While devoting my attention mainly to Catherine's own work and influence upon the politics of her age, I have endeavored at the same time to make my book a picture of certain aspects, religious and political, of the fourteenth century in Italy. In this undertaking, I have been aided greatly by the manuscripts still preserved of Catherine's letters, manuscripts full of unpublished matter that has been unaccountably neglected, having apparently escaped the notice of all of her previous biographers and editors. This material throws light upon every aspect of the saint's genius and has enabled me, at many points, to correct erroneously accepted ideas about the events of her life and the order of her writings.

From the very beginning, the biographical and historical value of Catherine's letters has been, to a considerable extent, impaired by copyists (and editors who followed them) omitting or suppressing passages that appeared to them to be of only temporary interest, or not tending immediately toward edification. A certain number appear to have been deliberately expurgated, in cases where the writer's burning words seemed likely to startle the susceptibilities of the faithful. This process seems to date back to the generation that immediately followed that of Catherine's original disciples.

A striking instance of this editorial suppression is seen in a certain letter that Aldo Manuzio (the editor of the second

edition of Catherine's letters, published in Venice in 1500) intro-
duces with the rubric: "To one whose name it is better not to
write, because of certain words used in the letter. Let not whoso
reads, or hears it read, wonder if the sense seems to him broken;
for where *et cetera* is written, many words are passed over, which
it is not meet that every one should know, nor even the name of
him to whom it went." Both these words and the omissions were
not made by Aldo himself. And the same heading then occurs
in every manuscript containing this letter that I have examined
and evidently dates back to the end of the fourteenth century.

Catherine was one of the greatest letter writers of her century.
Nearly four hundred of her letters have been preserved. They
are written to men and women in every walk of life and every
level of society. Her varied correspondents include a mendicant
in Florence, a Jewish banker
in Padua, and two sovereign
pontiffs and three kings. Leaders
of armies, rulers of Italian
republics, receive her burning
words and bow to her inspired
will, just as often as do private
citizens seeking her counsel in
the spiritual life, or simple monks
and hermits in their cells striving
to find the way of perfection.
She was able to warn a queen:
"Instead of a woman, you have
become the servant and slave of
nothingness, making yourself the
subject of lies and of the demon
who is their father," while she

An Update on Catherine's Letters

*Vida Scudder was in the process
of editing St. Catherine's letters for
English publication, simultaneous with
Gardner's writing of this biography.
Publication of the two books, within
two years of each other, gave birth to
the renaissance of St. Catherine scholarship that continued throughout the
twentieth century. Scudder begins her
introduction this way: "The letters
of Catherine Benincasa, commonly
known as St. Catherine of Siena, have
become an Italian classic; yet perhaps
the first thing in them to strike a reader
is their unliterary character. He only
will value them who cares to overhear
the impetuous outpourings of the heart*

4

and mind of an unlettered daughter of the people, who was also, as it happened, a genius and a saint. . . . Her letters were talked rather than written. She learned to write only three years before her death, and even after this time was in the habit of dictating her correspondence, sometimes two or three letters at a time, to the noble youths who served her as secretaries" (Scudder 1, 1). *More recently, another scholar has clarified, "Catherine's Letters amount at present, to 381. But it is not impossible that more might be found in old convent libraries or elsewhere"* (Cavallini, 7).

bids the wife of a tailor, "Clothe yourself in the royal virtues." Her wonderful, all-embracing and intuitive sympathy knows no barriers, but penetrates into the house of shame as well as into the monastery.

Some of the letters are purely mystical, ecstatic outpourings of Catherine's heart, the translation in ordinary speech of the conversation of angels, overheard in suprasensible regions. Others are nearer to familiar domestic correspondence, in which the daily needs of life become ennobled and even the innocent japery of her friends and followers isn't neglected.

Catherine's earliest letters were written for her by her women companions: Alessa, Cecca, and occasionally Giovanna Pazzi. During the heat of her greatest involvement in political affairs, she had three regular secretaries, three young nobles whom we will meet in the chapters to follow: Neri di Landoccio Pagliaresi, Stefano di Corrado Maconi, and Francesco di Messer Vanni Malavolti. Francesco Malavolti has left us a delightful picture of Catherine's method of composition at that time. We see her dictating simultaneously to these three young men three letters: one to Pope Gregory, another to Bernabo Visconti, and a third to a certain nobleman whose name Francesco doesn't remember. She dictates first to one, then to another. At times, her face is covered by her hands or veil, as though she is absorbed in thought; at other times with clasped hands and head raised up to heaven; and at intervals she seems rapt in ecstasy, but nevertheless goes on continuously speaking. Then suddenly, all three of the scribes stop writing, look puzzled, and appeal to Catherine for help. They have all taken down the same sentence, not knowing for whom it was intended. Catherine reassures them, saying, "Dear sons, don't trouble over this, for you have done it all by the work of the Holy Spirit. When the letters are finished, we will see how the words fit in with our intentions, and then we'll arrange what had best be done."

It was during a brief interval, between her leaving Florence and going to Rome during the late summer and early autumn of 1378, that Catherine had a few months of comparative peace in Siena and completed her great literary work, *The Dialogue of Divine Providence*. "When the peace was announced," writes Fra Raimondo (the book's compiler, and the author's spiritual director), "she returned to her own home and set herself with diligence to the task of composing a certain book, which was inspired by the supreme Spirit, and dictated in the vernacular. She had asked her secretaries to observe attentively at those times when she was rapt out of her corporeal senses, and to carefully write down whatever she would then dictate. They did this faithfully, and compiled a book full of high and salutary doctrines that had been revealed by the Lord and dictated to her." In her last letter, Catherine refers to it simply as *il libro nel quale io trovava alcuna recreazione*, "the book in which I found some recreation," even though her friends describe her as dictating it to the secretaries while "rapt in singular excess and abstraction of mind." It is not clear that Catherine herself would have made any claims of supernatural authority for the *Dialogue*, or would have regarded it as anything more than the pious meditations of a spirit "thirsty with great desire for the honor of God and the salvation of souls"—one who (in her own characteristic phrase)

6

"dwells in the cell of knowledge of self in order to better know the goodness of God."

The *Dialogue* was first published in the original Italian in Bologna in 1472, at Naples in 1478, and then in Venice in 1494. The *Dialogue* was translated into Latin by 1496 and then English by 1519.

The book is concerned with the whole spiritual life of a person in the form of a prolonged dialogue, or series of dialogues, between the eternal Father and the impassioned human soul, represented as Catherine herself. It opens with a striking passage on the essence of mysticism, the possibility of the union of the soul with God in love:

> When a soul lifts herself up, thirsty with great desire for the honor of God and the salvation of souls, she exercises herself for a while in habitual virtue and dwells in the cell of knowledge of self in order to better know the goodness of God. For love follows knowledge, and when she loves, she seeks to follow and to clothe herself with the truth. But in no way does the creature taste and become illumined by this truth as much as by means of humble and continuous prayer, based on knowledge of self and of God. Prayer exercises the soul in this way, by uniting her to God as she follows the steps of Christ crucified—and thus, by desire and affection and union of love, she is transformed into him. This seems to be what Christ meant when he said, "Those who love me will keep my word," and again, "those who love me will be loved by my Father, and I will love them and reveal myself to them" [Jn. 14:23, 21]. And in many places we find similar sentiments, by which we can see how the soul becomes another Christ, by affection and love.

The rest of the book is a practical expansion of the revelation that Catherine had in a vision after receiving Holy Communion on a feast of the Blessed Virgin in the autumn of the previous year. It is, as it were, a gathering together of the spiritual teachings scattered through her letters. On the whole, it reads somewhat less ecstatically, as though written with more deliberation than the letters, and is in parts drawn out to considerable length, sometimes moving slowly. The effect is of a mysterious voice from the cloud, talking on in a great silence, and the result is monotonous because the listener's attention becomes over-strained. Here and there, it is almost a relief when the divine voice ceases, and Catherine herself takes up the word. At other times, however, we feel that we have almost passed behind the veil that shields the Holy of Holies and that we are hearing Catherine's rendering into finite words the ineffable things she has learned by intuition.

Summary of the "Publication" of the Life of St. Catherine

Gardner offers the most succinct version of how Catherine's life came to be known in this paragraph from his original Catholic Encyclopedia article about her: "Among Catherine's principal followers were Fra Raimondo delle Vigne, of Capua (d. 1399), her confessor and biographer, afterwards General of the Dominicans, and Stefano di Corrado Maconi (d. 1424), who had been one of her secretaries, and became Prior General of the Carthusians. Raimondo's book, the 'Legend,' was finished in 1395. A second life of her, the 'Supplement,' was written a few years later by another of her associates, Fra Tommaso Caffarini (d. 1434), who also composed the 'Minor Legend,' which was translated into Italian by Stefano Maconi. Between 1411 and 1413 the depositions of the surviving witnesses of her life and work were collected at Venice, to form the famous 'Process.' Catherine was canonized by Pius II in 1461. The emblems by which she is known in Christian art are the lily and book, the crown of thorns, or sometimes a heart—referring to the legend of her having changed hearts with Christ. Her principal feast is on the 30th of April, but it is popularly celebrated in Siena on the Sunday following. The feast of her Espousals is kept on the Thursday of the carnival."

In dealing with the two great political struggles in which Catherine was engaged, I am indebted to the scholarship of Alessandro Gherardi, and to the masterly work of M. Noel Valois. I have, however, in many cases preferred to go directly to the original documents that deal with the Great Schism, still existing in the Archivio Segreto of the Vatican, by which I am able to give a somewhat full account of the origin of that extraordinary event. My grateful thanks are due to the authorities and officials of the Vatican Archives and Vatican Library, the Biblioteca Casanatense and Biblioteca Vittorio Emanuele at Rome, the Biblioteca Nazionale and Biblioteca Riccardiana of Florence, and the Biblioteca Comunale of Siena, for their kind assistance and courtesies.

CHAPTER ONE
Catherine's Hidden Life

Caterina Benincasa, whom we now call St. Catherine of Siena, was born on March 25, 1347—the Feast of the Annunciation, the first day of the new year as it was reckoned in those days in Italy. It had been 120 years since St. Francis had died at Assisi in the arms of Lady Poverty, his mystical bride, and a quarter of a century since Dante had passed away in exile at Ravenna. These two men are Catherine's elder brothers in the spirit. The seraphic father of Assisi, standard-bearer of the Crucified, as the voice in the high vision on Mount Verna had hailed him, is her predecessor in the mystical life. And Catherine is the *literary* successor of the poet of the *Divine Comedy* in the history of religious thought in Italy.

Among her famous contemporaries, Francesco Petrarca, or Petrarch in English, was nearly forty-three years old when Catherine was born. Crowned as poet laureate six years earlier, he was then the literary dictator of Italy. It was probably in the year of Catherine's birth that he finished the first part of his *Canzoniere* (Song Book) for Madonna Laura, and began the second, nobler, and more spiritual series of lyrics with, "For, with death at my side, I seek a new rule for my life, and I see the better but cling to the worse."

Meanwhile, Giovanni Boccaccio was thirty-four years old, and not yet the author of the *Decameron*. He had written his early prose romance and poems, had deserted or been deserted by his Fiammetta, and was now either at Florence or, more likely, in Rome.

11

What Was Happening in Avignon?

Gardner mentions Pope Clement VI and the misrule of the church from Avignon, a city in southeastern France. This was the period known as the Avignon Papacy, when a succession of seven popes, all Frenchmen, ruled the church away from Rome during the fourteenth century; and then, in the early fifteenth century, "anti-popes" ruled from Avignon, during periods of time when there were actually more than one man claiming to St. Peter's throne. This era is generally known as the Great Western Schism. Catherine's life and influence had much to do with the problems of the papacy during her lifetime, and what happened in Avignon will play a large role throughout Gardner's telling of her story.

Geoffrey Chaucer, according to most of the theories of dating his birth, was a little boy of four to seven. King Edward III of England had won the battle of Crecy in the previous year. Charles of Luxembourg, King of Bohemia, had been elected Holy Roman Emperor as Charles IV. From Avignon, Pierre Roger de Beaufort misruled the Church of Christ and profaned the throne of the Fisherman, under the title of Pope Clement VI.

The condition of Italy had altered little since Dante wrote his famous lament in the sixth canto of the *Purgatorio*. She was not yet again "lady of provinces." "O wonderful poet," writes Catherine's contemporary, Benvenuto da Imola [author of a commentary on the *Divine Comedy*], "I wish that you would now come to life once again! Where is peace, where is liberty, where is tranquility in Italy? You would readily see, O Dante, that in your time certain particular evils oppressed her, but these, indeed, were small and few; for you enumerated among the woes of Italy the lack of a monarch and the discord of certain families, but now worse things oppress us." The Italian cities either groaned beneath the heavy yoke of sanguinary tyrants, or, if they still ruled themselves as free republics, were torn by internal dissensions and harassed by fratricidal wars with their neighbors. And the anarchy of the country was intensified

by the presence of the wandering companies of mercenary soldiers—Germans, Bretons, English, Hungarians—sometimes in
the pay of a despot, at others in the pay of a republic, but always
fighting for their own hands, levying large ransoms from cities
as the condition of not devastating their territory and exposing
the country people to the horrors of famine.

The moral state of the land matched the political. The
absence of the popes from Rome, the example of the evil lives
of the ministers of the church, the growing immorality of high
and low, were bringing religious life to a standstill in Italy. The
Franciscan revival was a thing of the past, while the encyclical
letters of the generals of the Dominicans testify to the deplorable degeneration of the Friars Preachers. There is abundant
evidence in the *Revelations* of Bridget of Sweden and in the
Dialogue of Catherine herself that moral corruption was rampant
in the convents and monasteries, among men and women alike.
Many of the secular priests openly kept concubines; others were
usurers; and many followed the example of that bishop recorded
by Dante in canto fifteen of the *Inferno* and did worse. The spirit
of worldliness, of wickedness in high places, stalked unabashed
through the church, while the three beasts of Dante's allegory
made their dens in the papal court.

In the year after Catherine's birth, 1348, the great pestilence
swept over Italy, Provence, France, and Spain, and in the following year spread to England and the rest of Europe. It was said
that the Black Death was brought to Europe in the galleys of two
Genoese ships. The scourge did not rage throughout Italy with
equal violence; Milan and other cities near the Alps suffered
comparatively little, while Florence and Siena endured its worst
horrors. For the five months that it devastated these two cities,
from April or May until the beginning or end of September,

13

Blessed Bernardo Tolomei
(1272–1348)

One of the more fascinating charac-
ters of the early fourteenth century,
Bernardo (he took the name in honor of
St. Bernard of Clairvaux) was from a
wealthy family, educated early by the
Dominicans but not formally received
by them, spent time as a soldier for the
Germans, and worked in the Sienese
government, before praying to the
Blessed Virgin to improve his eyesight.
He was miraculously cured and then
dedicated himself to an ascetic and
monastic-style life. He moved about ten
miles out of town, began living accord-
ing to the Rule of St. Benedict, and
quickly gained followers. An abbey
was formed by 1313, known as the
Abbey of Monte Oliveto Maggiore. It
is still one of the largest in Tuscany.

all civic life was suspended, and about four-fifths of the population perished. Peculiarly appalling is the account given by the Sienese chronicler, Agnolo di Tura. Men and women felt the fatal swelling and suddenly, and while they spoke, would fall dead. Without any ecclesiastical ceremony, the abandoned dead were thrown indiscriminately into great trenches hastily dug in different parts of the city, and covered up with a little earth to keep them from the dogs. "And I, Agnolo di Tura, called Grasso, buried five of my sons in one trench with my own hands."

People said, in those days, that the end of the world had come. Bernardo Tolomei, the founder of the Benedictines known as Olivetani, came down with his white-robed monks from the security of secluded Monte Oliveto to labor among the sufferers in the streets of Siena and other Tuscan cities; with many of his brothers, he died in the work. Bernardo had fewer imitators in his own city than among the Florentines. Matteo Villani tells us that in Florence many who devoted their lives to the service of the plague stricken either escaped entirely or, if they took the infection, recovered, and their example encouraged others to similar efforts. To him it seemed like a second universal deluge, sent as a divine punishment for the sins of the world. During the decade preceding the pestilence, the population of Florence was between

120,000 and 125,000; the survivors numbered not more than 30,000. It was indeed a black flood of some sort, severing the Italy that had been Dante's from the Italy that was to be Catherine's.

At about this same time, Boccaccio was apparently in Naples, where he began his *Decameron* with the rhetorical description of the pestilence at Florence, the details of which he had not personally witnessed. The horrors had no good effect on people's minds, and those who believed that a great renovation of the world would come were quickly disillusioned. Restraint and convention were cast off; what followed was riot and excess among the survivors. The deserted streets rang with the shout of revelers or echoed to the fierce grasp on people's souls. "Without any restraint," writes Matteo Villani, "almost all our city plunged into evil living, and the same and worse did the other cities of the world." Scarcity and famine followed in many places, and work was kept at a standstill. Dissensions and quarrels arose over questions of heritage and succession. The cynical and shameless stories of the *Decameron* paint the corruption of the following years with a master's hand. There is surely exaggeration, and there is the writer's hatred of the priests and their allies, but the reader of certain terrible chapters of Catherine's *Dialogue*, written only thirty years later, will find a striking confirmation of Boccaccio's testimony.

The Black Death in Siena

Gardner offers numbers to illustrate the effect of the Black Death on the city of Florence. Estimates for Siena are even more dire. "Suddenly during the summer months of 1348 more than half the inhabitants of Florence and Siena died of the bubonic plague. . . . Siena was reduced from around 42,000 to 15,000. Never before or since has any calamity taken so great a proportion of human life. The plague struck again in 1363 and once more in 1374, though it carried off far fewer people than in the terrible months of 1348. The survivors were stunned. The Sienese chronicler Angolo di Tura tells of burying his five children with his own hands. 'No one wept for the dead,' he says, 'because every one expected death himself'" (Meiss, 65).

15

The house in which Catherine was born still stands, even though it has been transfigured, not irreverently or impiously, by generations of worshipers. It stands on the side of the third of Siena's hills that rise opposite the Duomo over the deep and fragrant Vallepiatta, the hill that is crowned by the great red-brick church of the Friars Preachers, San Domenico. Catherine's family belonged to the class and faction known as the *Dodicini*, the people that then ruled and governed the city of Siena. Her father, Giacomo di Benincasa, was a dyer, a simple and God-fearing citizen, pure in heart and gentle in speech, such a one as Giotto or Simone Martini might have painted. Her mother, Lapa di Puccio di Piagente, was the daughter of a citizen of the same class of life who seems to have also been a poet.

At the time of Catherine's childhood, her father was a fairly rich man and the family all lived together in the house where his workshop was located. That part of Siena is still redolent with the aroma of the dyers' and tanners' labors, and the strange, pleasant smell links the past and present of the people of the city. Lapa bore Jacomo a very large family of children. We have the names of five sons: Benincasa, Bartolomeo, Sandro, Niccolo, and Stefano; and five daughters who were older than Catherine: Niccoluccia, Maddalena, Bonaventura, Lisa, and Nera. Such was the refined purity of the atmosphere of the dyer's house that when Bonaventura, the third daughter, married, she was so appalled by the

---

Who Was Friar Raimondo?

This is the second instance where Raimondo and his Legenda are mentioned. Raimondo delle Vigne (ca. 1330–99) and Catherine were good friends. He was one of her confessors and confidantes, as well as her first biographer. Of noble birth, Raimondo (often anglicized to Raymond of Capua—the place of his birth) became a Dominican while a law student in Bologna. Gardner quotes from the Legenda—also known in English as The Life of Saint Catherine of Siena— throughout his biography.

---

licentiousness of the conversation of her husband and his young friends that she fell seriously ill and was only restored to health by her husband's conversion. This Bonaventura was Catherine's favorite sister. A twin sister, christened Giovanna, was born at the same time as Catherine, but died shortly after. From her birth, Catherine—who was the only one of her younger children that Lapa was able herself to nourish—was the chief darling and most beloved of her mother out of all the family. She is usually stated to have been the youngest, but Raimondo's *Legenda* states: "After Lapa had brought forth Catherine, she gave birth to another girl who was called Giovanna, to renew the memory of the departed sister of Catherine; and this was the last, after she had given birth to twenty-five children." This second Giovanna, or Nanna, died when Catherine was sixteen years old, in April 1363.

As she grew up, the young Catherine became the darling of her district. "Truly," writes Friar Raimondo, "the wisdom and prudence of her talk, the sweetness of her holy conversation, no tongue or pen could easily describe. Those alone know it who experienced it. Not only her speech but also her whole bearing had a strange power, whereby the minds of people were drawn to good and to delight in God, that all sadness was excluded from the hearts of those who conversed with her, and every mental weariness was driven out; even the memory of all troubles departed, and so a great tranquility of soul took its place, so that each one, marveling at himself, rejoiced with a new sort of joy, saying in his mind: It is good for me to be here, let me make three tabernacles." Many in Siena felt such delight in Catherine's childish wisdom and in her company.

To such a child, in such an age, visions began to come as a matter of course. She was only six years old when she returned with her brother Stefano from the house of their sister

Bonaventura, looked up, and saw over the summit of the church of San Domenico, Christ seated on an imperial throne, clad in the papal robes and wearing a tiara, attended by Sts. Peter and Paul and the beloved disciple, John. He smiled upon her and blessed her, and she was absorbed in ecstasy. She didn't know where she was until her brother, calling and pulling her by the hand, brought her back to Earth.

It was at this time that Catherine became more silent, and she began to abstain from food and to afflict her own flesh. She wandered in the woods and caves in order to imitate the ancient anchorites of the desert. She dreamed of entering the Dominican Order in the disguise of a boy. She gathered other little girls of the same age around her, to join in her prayers and discipline themselves together with her. Burning more and more with the fire of divine love every day, she consecrated her virginity to Christ. In later years, she told her confessors that all of this happened when she was only seven.

However, when Catherine had passed the age of twelve and was considered marriageable according to the customs of Siena, her sister Bonaventura, to whom she could refuse nothing, persuaded her at their mother's instigation to change her mode of life for a while. She dyed her hair and adorned her body, dressing becomingly, and conformed with the fashions of their little world. She complained bitterly about this later on, as a grievous sin, and did heavy penance for it, accusing herself of having loved her sister more than God. Even the comfortable exhortations of Friar Raimondo couldn't make her see it in any other light. Bonaventura died in August 1362, and Catherine immediately returned to her former mode of life. However, her father and brothers would have none of it, especially after the death of the elder sister, whose husband had been a man of some importance. They insisted upon finding a husband for Catherine whose alliance would strengthen the position of their family in the city. But finding her obstinate and undutiful, they had recourse to a certain friar of San Domenico named Tommaso della Fonte. He had been brought up in their house and was probably a relation of one of Catherine's other sisters' husbands.

This Friar Tommaso is the first of those sons of St. Dominic that Catherine came to know. The Dominicans were a group of worthy men who, in the midst of all the ecclesiastical corruption that surrounded them, maintained their single-hearted faith and religious fervor unimpaired, and found in the scholasticism of Thomas Aquinas sufficient answer for all the problems of those days. Friar Tommaso was Catherine's first confessor, and seems to have written some account of her life that was later incorporated into Raimondo's great *Legenda*.

Finding Catherine resolute, Tommaso encouraged her to follow her inspiration, and counseled her to cut off her beautiful hair as a sign to her family that her intention was fixed. The inevitable domestic persecution followed. Catherine's room was taken from her and she was compelled to do all the menial drudgery of the house, so that she would have neither the time nor place for prayer and devotion. They heaped abuse and reproaches upon her in order to break her obstinacy. But it was all in vain. Thrown back upon herself, the girl invented the refuge that she was later to urge upon her followers that they, too, should find—and that could never be taken from them: the cell of self-knowledge. According to the *Legenda*, "She made herself in her mind, by inspiration of the Holy Spirit, a secret cell, out of which she resolved never to go by reason of any external occupation." And, "She told me that she firmly pictured to herself that her father represented Our Lord and Savior Jesus Christ; her mother the most glorious Mother of God; and that her brothers and the rest of the household were the holy apostles and disciples. And because of this imagination, she served them all with great gladness and diligence. Everyone marveled."

She had more visions during this time, as well. In one dream she thought she saw St. Dominic holding in one hand a white lily, which burned and was not consumed like the bush seen by Moses; in the other hand, the saint was offering her the black and white habit of the Dominican tertiaries, the Sisters of Penance.

By this time, her father became convinced that his daughter's conduct had a higher sanction, and wasn't prompted by mere childish caprice. He had come upon her secretly one day as she prayed in the room of her brother Stefano (the only brother who was still unmarried), and had seen a snow-white dove hovering over her head. And so, when the girl, ordinarily bashful and silent, suddenly revealed to the family her vow and her unalterable resolution of having Christ alone for her Spouse, her father told her to follow the inspiration of the Holy Spirit, for she would meet with no opposition from him. As Raimondo tells it, "Then, having obtained this full and long-desired freedom to serve God, the virgin, already entirely dedicated to Him, began zealously to order all her life in the divine service. She asked and obtained a small room separate from the others in which she could devote herself to God and afflict her body according to her desire. . . . In this little chamber were renewed the old works of the holy fathers of Egypt, and all the more wondrously, without any human teaching, example, or guidance."

In order to make this freedom still more secure, Catherine soon took the habit of the Sisters of Penance of St. Dominic, called in Italy the Mantellate—the white robe of innocence and the black mantle of humility, in which we still see her clad in pictures. These Mantellate were not nuns, strictly speaking, but devoted themselves to the service of God in their own homes.

At first, the Sisters refused to receive a maiden into their number, as their order was then composed only of widows; but after a while, when Catherine lay ill and assured her mother that God and St. Dominic would take her from the world if her desire was not fulfilled, they told Lapa they would accept Catherine, provided that the girl was not too beautiful. They accepted her as a Sister, and on her recovery to health, she received the habit from one of the Dominican friars who acted as director of the sisterhood at San Domenico in the Cappella delle Volte—that little chapel still so fragrant with her spirit. There is some small difference of opinion as to the date of her taking the habit, but I think it was most likely about the beginning of 1363.

The Beginning of Her Asceticism

Then began that life of almost incredible austerity and mystical communings with the unseen that made the whole existence of this young maiden of the people seem a new, unheard-of miracle. Gradually abstaining from one thing after another, Catherine freed herself from all dependence on food or sleep. In a short while, she could easily restrict herself to raw herbs, a little bread, and water. Then the bread was left out and she ate only the herbs. Soon, even that became a torment to her and she seems often to have lived only on the Blessed Sacrament. "In the time during which I was allowed to be the witness of her life," writes Fra Raimondo, "she lived without any nourishment of food or drink. Aided by no natural power, she ever sustained, with joy, pains and labors that would have been insupportable to others." While these things seemed miracles to Fra Raimondo and his friends, we know that others, of no less repute in the spiritual life, cried out against them.

In her later years, during the time of her association with Raimondo, she would sometimes drink and eat a little in order to avoid scandal. On one occasion, Catherine appears to have asked the pope to impose a rigid fast of bread and water on her, as a condition of gaining an indulgence. She also slept on a bare board. At first she wore a hair shirt, but dreading the least trace of uncleanliness, she changed it for a chain of steel, which she fastened so tightly around her sides that it pierced the skin and lacerated her tender flesh. Toward the end of her life, Raimondo compelled her, by holy obedience, to lay it aside, which she did, although unwillingly.

Catherine gradually became one of those saints, horrible and repulsive in the eyes of many in an age that worships material gain and physical comfort, who have offered themselves as a sacrifice to the Eternal Justice for the sins of the world. Gradually, she overcame the need for sleep, until she would sometimes have only a half hour in the space of two days and two nights—and this she told her confessor was the hardest of all her victories of this kind. She especially loved to keep watch in prayer continuously while the friars of San Domenico, whom she called her *brothers*, slept, and then rest a little on her hard board when they rose for Matins. Not content with this, she would scourge herself with a little steel discipline until the blood ran down from her shoulders to her feet. "Three times a day, she shed the blood from her body to render to her Redeemer blood for blood," writes Raimondo. She who had been a robust child became so attenuated and wasted that it seemed a wonder that the ardent spirit could still be confined in so immaterial a prison. Her mother implored her in vain to mitigate her austerities. On one occasion when Lapa convinced her daughter to accompany her to the famous hot baths in the area, Catherine waited until she was unobserved and then exposed her flesh to the flow of the boiling water, meditating on the torments of hell and purgatory as she experienced the pain.

There have been other women who have done similar things at different times in the history of the church—especially in times of the greatest corruption—but more frequently in the seclusion of the cloister or in the poor hovels of the peasantry. Catherine differs from these others, such as St. Fina of San Gimignano and St. Lydwine of Schiedam and St. Rose of Lima, in that asceticism was only a small portion of her life's work.

Catherine was prepared to endure the pains of hell for the salvation of others. "How could I be content, Lord," she prayed, "if any one of those who have been created in your image and likeness, even as I, should perish? If your truth and justice permitted it, I would want hell to be completely destroyed, or at least that no soul should ever again descend into it. And if I were put over the mouth of hell to close it, so that no one should ever again enter it, I would rejoice, because all of my neighbors would be saved." And on another occasion she prayed: "Lord,

Asceticism in Catherine's Life

This is the second time that Gardner's account refers to Catherine afflicting her body in devotion to God. This aspect of medieval spirituality troubles many people today, and not without good reason. Still, it is important to understand where it originated: the Gospels tell of Christ himself denying himself, enduring times of hunger and thirst. It should also be noted that people of late medieval times didn't view things like flagellation and burning at the stake with the horror that we do today. These were people who believed that the soul was clearly more important than the body. Many of the same people who were willing to burn their enemies were also active in punishing their own bodies as a spiritual practice.

give me all the pains and infirmities that there are in the world, to bear in my body. I am ready to offer you my body in sacrifice, and to bear all for the world's sins, so that you may spare it and change its life to another."

Her Visions and Teachings

Catherine entered a prolonged retreat after she received the Dominican habit. For three continuous years she kept a complete silence, speaking only with her confessor, Fra Tommaso della Fonte, and occasionally with other persons at his insistence. She dwelled continually within the religious enclosure of her little cell, never leaving it unless it was to go to Mass. In Fra Raimondo's poetical phrase, "She found the desert within her own house and solitude in the midst of people."

Then her continuous series of visions began. In her narrow cell she smelled the fragrance of celestial lilies, and she heard the ineffable melodies of paradise, sweetest of all on the lips of those who had loved Christ on Earth with the most ardent love. "Father," she said to Fra Tommaso, "don't you hear the Magdalene, how she sings with a high voice and with grace of singular sweetness?" Christ himself appeared to her spiritual eyes, instructed her in the secret mysteries of the Divinity, conversed continually with her as friend to friend, and kissed her.

At the very beginning of these visions and revelations, the Lord delivered to her the simple doctrine that became the basis of her whole conception of God and humanity: "Do you know, O daughter, who you are and who I am? You are she who are not, and I am he who is. If you have this knowledge in your soul, the enemy will never be able to deceive you, and you will escape from all his snares; never will you consent to anything against my commandments, and every grace, every truth, every clearness, you will acquire without difficulty."

"The soul," Catherine said in illustration of this, "that already sees her own nothingness and knows that all her good is in her Creator, entirely abandons herself with all her powers and all creatures, and immerges herself utterly in her Creator. . . . She doesn't see other crea-

A Mystic's Cell

"To many medieval hermits, the cell seems to have implied no extreme degree of ascetic seclusion, but the 'simple life,' disentangled from worldly cares, pursued under strict religious rule, yet not inconsistent with normal human relations, tempered interest in public affairs, and scholarly pursuits." (Scudder 2, x)

tures or herself, but only God. She doesn't remember herself or them, but only God. One who dives down into the sea, and is swimming under the water, does not see or touch anything but the water and the things that are in the water; he sees nothing outside those waters, touches nothing, feels nothing. If things outside of the water reflect themselves in the water, the diver can see them, but only in reflection. This is the ordered and right love of self and of all creatures, in which we cannot go wrong, because it is governed of necessity by divine rule. By this rule, nothing is desired outside God because it is exercised in God and is ever in him."

From this, too, Catherine derived her doctrine of holy hate. The more a soul is conjoined with God, the more it hates the offenses that she commits against him. And seeing that the origin of every sin has its roots in the sensual parts, the soul is inspired to a holy hatred of this, and wages a relentless war of the spirit against it. "Woe to the soul," says Catherine, "where this holy hatred is not to be found. Where it is not, self-love will reign, which is the sink-hole of all sins and the root and cause of every evil." Upon this doctrine her whole teaching may be said to depend.

Catherine explained all of this in detail to an English friar, William Flete, about nine or ten years later. At the beginning of 1376 he recounted, "The holy mother, speaking of herself in the third person, said that at the beginning of her illumination she set as the foundation of her life against self-love, the stone of self-knowledge, which she distinguished into three, small stones. The first was the consideration of creation, that is, that she had no being of herself, but was dependent entirely upon the Creator for both production and conservation, done entirely through his grace and mercy. The second was the consideration of redemption, that is, how the Redeemer had restored the life of grace that had been destroyed, through his pure and fervent love that humanity had done nothing to deserve. The third was the consideration of her own sins, committed after baptism and the grace received by it, for which she had deserved eternal damnation. From these three considerations there was born in her so great a hatred of herself that she desired nothing according to her own will, but only according to the will of God. From this it followed that she was

Would Catherine Be Considered a Masochist Today?

Perhaps. Certainly, many today would consider Catherine to have an eating disorder; but one scholar provides a helpful distinction: "If so much as a bean remained in Catherine of Siena's stomach, she vomited. . . . In describing this behavior as 'holy anorexia' I mean to draw attention to both the similarities and the differences between it an 'anorexia nervosa.' The modifier is the key; whether anorexia is holy or nervous depends on the culture in which a young woman strives to gain control of her life. . . . The modern anorexic exhibits visual distortion and literally sees herself in the mirror as being heavier and wider than she is. . . . The holy anorexic sees Jesus' bridal ring on her finger and a place for herself in heaven; she feels God's love and energetically lives on the host alone" (Bell, 20). Also, it was common for medieval women mystics to exhibit this sort of behavior when it came to food and eating. Religious scholar Caroline Bynum wrote a landmark book, Holy Feast and Holy Fast, on this subject two decades ago. She summarized three common patterns in the way that

26

content with every tribulation and temptation, not only because they came to her by the will of God, but also to see herself punished and chastised. She began to have the greatest displeasure from those things in which she previously had delighted, and a great delight in what had previously displeased her."

But as Catherine's conversations with God grew more frequent and familiar, so did the

medieval women mystics, such as St. Catherine, related to food: "Women fast, women feed others, and women eat (but never ordinary food). Women fast—and hunger becomes an image for excruciating, never-satiated love of God. Women feed—and their bodies become an image of suffering poured out for others. Women eat—and whether they devour the filth of sick bodies or the blood and flesh of the eucharist, the foods are Christ's suffering and Christ's humanity with which one must join before approaching triumph, glory, or divinity" (Bynum, 186).

manifestations of the evil of the world press themselves upon her. And, as men and women of the Middle Ages often gave evil a personal and anthropomorphic form in the shape of temptations of the devil, so did Catherine. At first, she doubted whether the visitation that seemed celestial might not, in reality, have some sort of diabolical source. We read in Book I, chapter nine of the *Legenda:* "But I will teach you," said the Voice in her heart, "how to distinguish my visions from the visions of the enemy. My vision begins with terror, but always, as it grows, gives greater confidence. It begins with some bitterness, but always grows more sweet. In the vision of the enemy the opposite happens; in the beginning it seems to bring some gladness, confidence, or sweetness, but as it proceeds, fear and bitterness grow in the soul." And it continues, "I will give you another sign, as well, more infallible and certain: Since I am truth, there always results from my visions a greater knowledge of truth in the soul, and . . . it is inevitable that from my visions the soul becomes more humble, knowing herself better and despising her own

27

sinfulness. In the visions of the enemy the opposite happens. Since he is the father of lies, and the king over all the children of pride, his visions result in the soul a certain self-esteem or presumption, which is the proper office of pride. . . . For truth always makes the soul humble, but the lie makes her proud."

There came a time, toward the end of three years, when these assaults of the enemy became horrible and unbearable. Spirit men and women, using obscene words and even more obscene gestures, seemed to invade her little cell, sweeping around her like the souls of the damned in Dante's *Inferno*. Their suggestions grew so hideous and persistent that she fled in terror from her cell and took refuge in the church. But then they pursued her there, as well. It was then that Christ seemed far away from her. She cried out, "I have chosen suffering for my consolation and will gladly bear these and all other torments, in the name of the Savior for as long as it shall please him." The *Legenda* tells the story: "When she said this, all the assembly of demons departed in confusion and a great light appeared from above, illuminating the room. In the light, the Lord Jesus himself, nailed to the cross and stained with blood, called to the holy virgin saying, 'My daughter Catherine, do you see how much I have suffered for you? Let it not be hard, then, for you to endure for me.' Then he approached her to console her, and spoke sweetly to her of the triumph that she had already won. But Catherine, like St. Antony before her, said, 'But where were you, Lord, while my heart was tormented with so much foulness?' To which the Lord answered, 'I was in your heart. You, my daughter, have now merited even greater favor from me. From here forward, I will reveal myself to you more often and in more familiar ways.'" This was the first time that the divine voice called her by her name, and it gave her such delight that she asked her confessor, Fra Tommaso, if he would always address her in this way: *My daughter Catherine,* so that the sweetness would always be renewed.

Her colloquies with the Savior grew more frequent, prolonged, and intimate. Sometimes he appeared to her with his Virgin Mother, sometimes with St. Dominic, Mary Magdalene, John the Evangelist, Paul, or other saints. "But most times," as Raimondo's *Legenda* tells us, "he came unattended and conversed with her as a friend with a most intimate friend, in such a way that (as she herself secretly and bashfully confessed to me) the Lord and she recited the Psalms, walking up and down in her room, as two religious clerics may say the Divine Office together. What a wondrous, marvelous, and unheard of demonstration of the divine familiarity!"

During this time of seclusion, Catherine learned to read. Fra Raimondo tells us that she originally got the alphabet from a companion of hers, but found it so hard to get further that, fearing she was losing time, she prayed to God and was miraculously instructed. When he knew her, she could read any writing, rapidly and with ease. Reading, however, was not her only recreation. She took great delight in flowers of all kinds and would weave them into crosses and garlands in her spare time, singing mystical songs of divine praise. She would send or give these as presents, either directly or through Fra Tommaso della Fonte. A young Dominican friar, Tommaso di Antonio Caffarini, soon to be closely associated with her spiritual life, tells us that, before he knew her, he had received some of these mystical gifts through her confessor.

At the same time, perhaps inevitably, her ecstasies were growing on her. After Holy Communion, or at other times when meditating on the mysteries of God, she would be rapt out of her senses for a while, her body rigid and seeming lifeless, insensible to

Catalepsy and Epilepsy

In Catherine's day, afflictions such as catalepsy and epilepsy were considered by most people to be signs of demon possession. Catalepsy is characterized by rigid muscles and an immovable posture; the afflicted will enter this state seemingly unknowingly and unwillingly, only to return from it moments or minutes later (easily compared to hypnotism). Epilepsy is more common and better understood by physicians; it is a neurological disorder characterized by seizures. Even though epileptics were often persecuted in the ancient and medieval eras, the disease became popularly associated with greatness and even sanctity in the seventeenth and eighteenth centuries. It was called the "sacred disease," and was said to have possibly afflicted religious figures such as St. Bridget of Sweden, Joan of Arc, and in the last century, St. Thérèse of Lisieux.

touch. This increased with years and lasted throughout her life. There are many people today who would regard this simply as a form of catalepsy, and who will see in much of these visionary experiences little more than hysterical phenomena. The faithful followers of St. Catherine today need not deny that this is possible, or even probable. In the record of her revelations, we are confronted with things that are incapable of literal acceptance—things that, at times, even offend our religious sensibilities, occurring side by side with profound truths, expressed with wonderful precision and startling inspiration. In the lives of many of the great mystical saints, phenomena connected with organic hysteria existed side by side with the possession of a suprasensible revelation. It has even been argued, in the case of St. Teresa of Avila, that organic hysteria and knowledge of the workings of her own soul were so clear and exact that she could distinguish perfectly between these two classes of experiences, the natural and the supernatural, and that this fact is the strongest guarantee for the truth of her account of the latter.

Catherine, like Teresa, had a practical sense as well as angelic wisdom. With her unwavering fortitude and calm resolution, she was poles away from a hysterical subject. Still, perhaps, with all her celestial endowments, this thing was given to her as the Pauline "thorn in the flesh, a messenger from Satan to batter me." She learned early how to discriminate between the two kinds of visions, those that proceeded from her divine teacher and those that were the work of the father of lies. But I don't think she could distinguish between the natural and the supernatural in the way that has been claimed for St. Teresa. At times, in her visions, we cannot miss apparent hallucinations, to which a physician would probably assign a hysterical origin.

Spiritual Marriage

The mystical revelations and divine colloquies of these three years culminated in the "spiritual marriage" of Catherine with Christ on the last day of the carnival, most probably, I think, in the year 1366. By "spiritual marriage," the mystics clearly mean something different, not in degree but in kind, from what every nun may be said to experience when she consecrates her virginity to Christ. They seem to hold that some chosen souls, after passing through purgation and illumination, having been tried in tribulation and mortification and enlightened by profound meditation, attain to a state of mystical perfection. This "spiritual marriage" includes an intellectual vision of Christ in the soul, and they become united to him in some peculiarly absorbing manner, becoming, in some way, *one* with him.

It seems that Catherine did not regard spiritual marriage as St. Teresa and St. John of the Cross understand it, as attainable in this world—at least not for one like her, who was walking with Christ and talking with him while in the midst of the world, still called to a life of active labor for his name rather than to sheer contemplation. Her spiritual marriage was to have its mystical consummation in the eternal nuptials of paradise. "It would be foolish," writes St. John of the Cross, "to think that the language of love and the mystical intelligence can be explained in words of any kind."

Catherine had prayed again and again, Fra Raimondo tells us, for the gift of perfection in the virtue of faith, so that it would never be shaken or beaten down by an assault of the enemy. She always heard the same answer: "I will espouse you to myself in faith." After a time, while all Siena was given up to the usual festivities on the last day of the carnival season, the voice told her that the time had come: "I will celebrate solemnly today with you the festival of marriage of your soul, and even as I promised, I will espouse you to myself in faith." Raimondo adds: "While the Lord was still speaking there appeared the most glorious Virgin, his mother, the most blessed John the Evangelist, the glorious apostle Paul, and the most holy Dominic, the father of her order. Together with these, the prophet David, who had set the psalter to music in his hands, played the sweetest melody, as the Virgin Mother took the right hand of Catherine and guided her to her Son. Graciously consenting to his mother, the only begotten of God drew out a ring of gold which had a circle of four pearls enclosing a most beautiful diamond, and placed the ring upon the ring-finger of Catherine's right hand. . . . Then the vision disappeared, but that ring always remained on her finger, not so that others could see it, but only for herself. She often, with bashfulness, confessed to me that she always saw that ring on her finger; there was never a time when she didn't see it."

CHAPTER TWO

From Dante to Saint Catherine

To understand Catherine's political work and mission, we must turn to the states and rulers that most concerned her. The "Babylonian Captivity" of the popes at Avignon, which began with Clement V in 1305, was still to some extent the dominant feature of the religious landscape. It was on Clement's death in 1314 that the voice had been heard of "a man who was a prophet," as Dante said in his letter to the Italian cardinals at Carpentras, and had renewed for Rome the lamentation of Jeremiah for Jerusalem.

Things had grown worse under Clement's successor, John XXII (1316–34). "The gold that is the holiness of virtues has grown dim in the Church," wrote Alvarus Pelagius, "for everyone covets material gold. Ordinations and sacraments are bought and sold for gold. Whenever I entered the apartment of the Pope, I saw brokers and tables full of gold, and clerics counting and weighing florins." Petrarch wrote two poetical letters to Benedict XII (1334–42), pleading with him to return to Italy, and he offered a similar appeal in the name of Rome to the man who now sat on the papal throne, Clement VI (1342–52). In Clement VI, the corruption of this era of the papacy was personified. Learned, eloquent, and magnanimous, his private life was scandalous. The luxury and prodigality of his court was so extreme that he would have taxed all Christendom if he had been able to. He wasted the treasures of the church by lending money to the French kings, aiding them in their wars against England. He filled the College of Cardinals with men of his own stamp and country, godless and worldly, many of them also living evil lives. If Petrarch is to be believed, the riotous licentiousness of these younger cardinals was only matched by the senile debauchery of their elders who also wore that hat, in Dante's phrase, "which does pass from bad vessel to worse." "Our two Clements," said a French prelate of the papal curia to Petrarch, "have destroyed more of the Church in a few years than seven of your Gregories could restore in many centuries."

On December 2, 1352, the campanile of St. Peter's was struck by lightning. All the bells were dashed to the ground and fused together as though they had been melted in a furnace. A report quickly spread through Rome that Pope Clement VI was dead. Christ said in the heart of a widow, who later became St. Bridget of Sweden, "Now the bells are burning, and men are crying out: Our lord is dead, our lord the Pope has departed. Blessed be this day, but not blessed that lord. How strange, for where all should cry, 'May that lord live long and live happily,' instead they cry and say with joy, 'Down with him and may he not rise up again!' It is no wonder, for he who should have cried, 'Come and you shall find rest for your souls,' instead cried, 'Come and behold me in pomp and ambition more than Solomon. Come to my court and empty your purses and you shall find perdition for your souls.'"

Giovanni Colombini

Clement's successor, Etienne d'Albret, took the title of Pope Innocent VI (1352–62). He was a simple man "of good life and not much knowledge," as one chronicle puts it, and he made an earnest but ineffectual attempt to reform the papal court. Amid this turmoil of political faction and moral corruption, men and women arose who looked for righteousness; flowers of the spiritual life bloomed even in the bloodstained streets of Siena and on the arid desert of the seven hills of Rome. Catherine's work was, to some extent, anticipated by the Swedish princess, Bridget, a flower of the north transplanted to the Eternal City by Giovanni Colombini, himself a Sienese.

Giovanni di Pietro Colombini was a rich merchant who belonged to the order of the Noveschi, also known as the Nine, an oligarchy of banking and mercantile interests that ruled Siena for about eighty years. In the third quarter of the thirteenth century, Siena enjoyed a period of considerable prosperity under the rule of these "good merchants of the Guelf party," the chief council or magistracy of the Nine. The Nine held office for two months, lived at the expense of the state, and were elected from the rich and enlightened burgher class. Giovanni was himself absorbed in mercantile pursuits and in the acquisition of wealth until one day, to soothe his irritation at dinner not being ready, his wife asked him to read a volume of the lives of the saints. He happened upon the legend of St. Mary of Egypt and was completely converted by reading it. Another of the Noveschi, or the Nine, Francesco di Mino Vincenti, joined him and they went to consult with the pious Carthusian, Pietro Petroni, who told them to follow Christ in the most absolute poverty. This appears to have happened in 1355. A few years later, they carried out Pietro's advice and

Giovanni Colombini

"Colombini resembled the Saint of Assisi in many ways. They both underwent a complete revolution of spirit; their mission was purely a lay mission; they had the same contempt for honors and riches; their high respect for womanly friendship in religion was identical, and they were both possessed of the same fervent spirit of charity and of respect for ecclesiastical jurisdiction. This latter spirit of submission to authority was in contrast to those 'heretical' sects of Rome which did homage to poverty, not so much for the sake of self-sacrifice as for the sake of pride in their poverty, which they paraded like a flag of rebellion." (Misciattelli, 74–75)

Who Were the *Poverelli?*

The poverelli *movement originated with the original Poverello ("poor little man"), St. Francis of Assisi. In fact, most of the* poverelli *were, like Francis, high-born sons and daughters who deliberately turned to poverty as an expression of spirituality. It was a way of mindful faith, to make oneself voluntarily poor, and to humble oneself sometimes in seemingly harsh ways. Poverelli reforms flamed up in the late medieval church from time to time, as a dramatic contrast to the frequent abuses of power and riches by the popes of that era.*

placed their daughters in the Benedictine monastery of Santa Bonda (of which the abbess was a sort of spiritual mother to this new movement) and gave away all their possessions to religion and the poor—Giovanni first making adequate provision for his wife.

Disciples came to them, who were received and clothed with rags at the Madonna of the Campo, and initiated into the spirit of these new *poverelli* by public humiliation through the streets of Siena— which one young noble who joined them confessed that he found as bitter as death. Among the earliest of these Jesuati (as their order was called) was Tommaso di Guelfaccio, one of the leading Noveschi, previously a man of soft and luxurious life, whom we will meet again in Catherine's circle.

Giovanni and Francesco then wandered over the Sienese *contado*, or county, preaching Christ and poverty, working everywhere a wonderful revival, stirring up a new life among the Franciscans and Dominicans themselves, who welcomed them with enthusiasm. One Franciscan friar said to Giovanni: "If religious people will once more begin to speak only of God, the spirit of holy fervor will return among us and we will set the world on fire!" Banished from Siena by the power of the day, they then wandered to Arezzo and other Tuscan cities, converting sinners, enforcing reparation of fame and goods, and healing feuds and factions. Pisa also gave them a glad welcome, and eventually the authorities of Siena, out of shame, revoked their sentence of banishment.

Something mystical lingers in the letters of Giovanni and Francesco from those days. But Bridget of Sweden, whose revelation on the death of Clement VI we have already heard, cuts a very different sort of figure. Born about the year 1303, Bridget was married to Ulf Gudmarsson, a Swedish man of noble birth, when she was still little more than a child. She bore him eight children and her married life was one of almost ideal happiness. Bridget worked for Christ and

The Gloom of the 1350s and 1360s

"The years following the Black Death were the most gloomy in the history of Florence and Siena, and perhaps of all Europe. The writing of the period, like the painting, was pervaded by a profound pessimism and sometimes a renunciation of life," writes Millard Meiss. Corpses began to appear in the edges of paintings, as did scenes of the tortures of hell, which were almost unknown in European art up until this time. Even the attitude of Christ toward the people seems to have changed: in frescos and other paintings throughout Tuscany, the figure of Christ appears angry, often punishing, in powerful poses, condemning of sinners, awesome and to be feared. (Meiss, 74–77)

the salvation of souls in the court of Magnus II, King of Sweden and Norway. She once requested that her confessor translate the Pentateuch into Swedish—and he did so. In 1343, she and Ulf took a pilgrimage to Santiago de Compostela, after which Ulf chose to become a monk, only to die in the following year.

Then the spirit of prophecy fell upon her, and the same mystical voice that later spoke to Catherine of Siena spoke in the heart of the Swedish princess. The wonderful book of *Revelations* that Bridget began to dictate is a spiritual autobiography, collection of letters, record of graces and visions, and a denunciation of the corruption of the times. It anticipates Catherine's letters as well as her *Dialogue*. For a while after Ulf's death, Bridget returned to the court in order to preach repentance there. A little later she founded her order of the Holy Savior, composed of men and women alike, each monastery containing two convents. But then she looked southward to Avignon and Rome, and the divine voice spoke in her heart again, inspiring her with an eloquent letter to Pope Clement to rebuke him as "a lover of the flesh," urging him to be converted before it was too late.

At the end of 1349, Bridget left Sweden for Rome. The desolation of the Eternal City struck deeply into her soul and inspired pages of pure eloquence worthy of Petrarch himself. A voice cried in her heart: "O Rome, your walls are broken down. Your gates are left unguarded. Your vessels are sold and your altars are desolate. The living sacrifice and morning incense are consumed in the outer courts and therefore the sweetest odor of sanctity no longer rises from the Holy of Holies." But still she saw room for hope. The holy voice told her, "You shall remain in Rome until you see the Pope and the Emperor, and you shall speak to them in my name the words that I will tell you." And so Bridget remained in Italy, mostly in Rome, tending the sick in hospitals and begging alms for the poor, while she waited for the promised advent of pontiff and emperor. Meanwhile, she had many revelations.

CHAPTER THREE
Catherine Enters into Her Vocation

It was probably in 1366 that Catherine of Siena began to leave her cell in order to join in the life of the family, and to begin working for the conversion of souls. The voice of God sounded in her ears, saying, "Open to me, my sister, my beloved, my dove," which Fra Raimondo interprets: "Open for me the gates of souls that I may enter them. Open the path by which my sheep may pass in and out and find pasture. Open for me your treasury of grace and knowledge and pour it out upon the faithful." The gifts that Catherine had received in her cell she was now to make manifest in the world.

Once more, Catherine devoted herself to all of the humblest, menial jobs around the house. With her father's permission, she had the freedom to come and go in service of others. She tended the sick both in their houses and in hospitals, employing great zeal in nursing even those afflicted by the most loathsome diseases. Catherine was herself afflicted with leprosy, which spread over her hands, after a period of time when she nursed a poor woman named Cecca who had been deserted by all others. But when the woman eventually died and Catherine prepared her body for burial, Catherine's body was miraculously healed.

To those who criticized her lack of eating, she would answer humbly, "God has smitten me for my sins with a singular infirmity, by which I am prevented from taking food. I would eat willingly, but I cannot. Pray for me so that God may forgive my sins." From early on, Catherine desired to be subject to others, even to the servant in her father's house, and the poor whom she encountered in the streets or in the hospital. In all sincerity, she regarded herself as the vilest of creatures and desired that others would treat her as such. Again and again we will find her asserting that her sins are the cause of the evil around her, and almost that she alone is responsible for the corruption of the world. There were times when she suffered needlessly through this humility.

Also from the beginning, she was persecuted and criticized by those with whom she was supposed to have joined in Christian ministry. Raimondo recounts, "She could hardly exercise an act of devotion in public without suffering criticisms, impediments and persecutions, particularly from those who ought to have protected and encouraged her in those very actions." Her sisters in religion slandered her and called on their superiors to correct her. They even gained some of the Dominican friars to their side, who refused to have any dealings with her, often deprived her of the blessed sacrament in communion, and even took away her faithful confessor for a time. At times, when they would allow her to worship in their church, they would also insist that she leave immediately afterward. This they did because Catherine would often pass into a state of ecstasy during which she might be unconscious for hours. On one occasion when they found her in this state, they forcibly threw her out of the church at midday and left her in the heat of the sun, watched over by some companions until she came to her senses. One friar even brutally kicked her as she lay helpless. Of course we are told that he later came to a dreadful death, as also did another friar of the same type: "religious in habit, but not in deeds." This other one, when the friars were in the choir of San Domenico after dinner, came down and pricked Catherine in many places with a needle. Catherine was not roused in the least from her trance, but afterward, she felt the pain in her body and perceived that someone had wounded her.

She found it most difficult to bear the affliction of being deprived the sacrament, with patience. Whenever she could, she communicated every day; this was the center of her inner life, but her bodily sustenance also seemed to depend on it. So great was her desire of being united to her celestial bridegroom in this way that it was physical, no less than mental agony, to be deprived of his embraces. "I am a miserable wretch," she wrote to one of her friars, "for my sins are so great, since you went away, that I have never been worthy to receive the most sweet and venerable Sacrament. Pardon my ignorance, father, and remember me at your most holy Mass and I will receive the body of the Son of God spiritually from you."

Not only her enemies, but even her confessor seemed sometimes to be against her. Fra Tommaso asked her, under the duty of obedience, to deny her visions and to regulate her life more like the lives of others around her. He did this particularly

A "Doctor of the Church"

Throughout his biography, Gardner uses Catherine's teachings (usually in epistolary form) to illuminate her life and the lives of others. These same teachings combined to create her legacy, and led to Pope Paul VI designating her a "Doctor of the Church" in 1970. Teresa of Avila and Catherine were the first women to hold this honor. In light of this, we may see Catherine's often ecstatic union with Christ as also an intellectual one. As Dante states, beatitude and the future joy of heaven, not to be enjoyed by all, are first experienced by a light in the mind: "Light intellectual replete with love, / Love of true good replete with ecstasy, / Ecstasy that transcendeth every sweetness" (Paradiso, canto XXX). Another commentator has recently offered this helpful explanation: "Catherine's method of doing theology can be described as a process whereby she, using her gifts of nature and grace, reflected prayerfully on what she received from others, developing it and clothing it with her own language, images and penetrative insights. In her manner of being a theologian she is an excellent example of the principle that any person genuinely trying to live the Christian life, who has an active faith and a reflective attitude, can do theology. In declaring the laywoman, Catherine of Siena, a Doctor of the Church, Paul VI is surely recognizing this principle" (O'Driscoll, 13).

41

in order to get Catherine to eat more. She always obeyed him humbly to the letter and she found agony in those attempts to eat and drink more often: "Let us go and execute this wretched sinner," she would say with a smile when the time came.

Her First Companions

Friends and disciples of both sexes began to gather around her at this time. Her little cell in her father's house became a center of religious life and a spiritual lamp to all in Siena who were looking for righteousness. A little group of Mantellate sisters became her constant companions. Chief among them were the two we still see supporting her in Giovanni Bazzi's glorious fresco: Alessa Saracini and Cecca (Francesca) Gori, both widows of noble birth who had given their possessions to the poor and taken the black and white habit of penance. The latter, an older woman, had three sons in the Dominican order, probably very young novices. The former, Alessa, was called by Fra Raimondo the most perfect and faithful of Catherine's disciples. Both Alessa and Cecca seem to have been educated women and to have written many of Catherine's letters for her.

Closely associated with these two were the saint's beloved sister-in-law, Lisa, the wife of her brother Bartolomeo. Catherine called her "my sister-in-law according to the flesh, but my sister in Christ." Catherine's own sister Lisa seems to also have taken the habit of a Dominican tertiary, as did another woman, named Caterina di Ghetto (or Scetto), who may have been the daughter of one of Catherine's brothers-in-law.

Her earliest male followers were two young Dominican friars. First was Fra Tommaso di Antonio Nacci Caffarini, not to be confused with the Fra Tommaso who was her early

The image of St. Catherine fainting or passing into a trance after receiving the Eucharist is one of the most common in her iconography. One of Giovanni Bazzi's (also known as Il Sodoma, in Italian art history) famous frescoes, painted in 1526 in Siena, depicts such a scene, dramatizing it further, as it is an angel who hands her the blessed sacrament. This work is called *Fainting and Ecstasy of St. Catherine* and can be found in the St. Catherine Chapel of San Domenico, along the right side of the nave.

confessor, a novice who was about seventeen years old. And second was Fra Bartolomeo di Domenico, slightly older and already a priest, who had been a companion in the novitiate with Fra Tommaso della Fonte, Catherine's early confessor. Next to Fra Raimondo, we owe most of our information about Catherine to the devotion of these two friars.

Fra Bartolomeo, for instance, gives us a detailed description of her cell, before she came out of it, while she conversed with no one except at the command or by the permission of her confessor. We see its door and window always closed, the hard couch of bare boards, the little lamps always burning day and night before the images of Christ, the Virgin, and the saints that were painted there. He tells us how all carnal passion died away when he approached her, and that others whose normal mode of thinking and feeling was quite alien from his own had the same experience: "For her aspect and address seemed to pour forth a certain fragrance of purity, more angelic than human, and through everything she was always joyful and merry." Nevertheless, there were certain things that Bartolomeo found hard to accept at first. He noticed that when she returned to consciousness after her prolonged ecstasies, Catherine always seemed to know what her women companions had done in the meanwhile, and she sometimes rebuked them for idle talk or waste of time. The friar, "in my stupidity, being still ignorant of the virtues of the holy virgin," could not always believe that she did this by what he calls the prophetic spirit. "But at that time, when I once came to her cell with her confessor, she asked us what we were doing the previous evening. Wanting to test her, we replied with a question of our own: 'What do you think?' And she answered, 'Who knows better than you yourselves?' Then her confessor rejoined, at my suggestion, 'I ask you, in obedience, to tell us if you know what we were doing.' But she humbly refused to do this. Then, her confessor asked it again. Bowing her head, Catherine said: 'You know well that there were four of you, and you were in the cell of the subprior talking for a long while at that late hour.' We asked her who the four were, and she named each of them; and we asked her what we said, and she recounted it. I was amazed but still assumed that one of us four had told her all of this. On the following day, I came to her and asked, 'Mother (for this is what we called her), how do you know what we do?' And she responded, 'Son, since it has pleased our sweet Savior to give me the sons and daughters that I have, nothing concerning you is hidden from me. He shows me clearly everything that is done about them.' Then I asked, 'Do you know, then, what I was doing yesterday evening?' And she said, 'Surely, for you were writing. Son, I always watch and pray for you. If you had good eyes, you would see me with you.'"

At first, Bartolomeo wasn't edified by her calling herself *miserable*, more wretched than all other people. He thought that she did not really mean what she said—until, to his question of how this could be, she answered as she did later on to Fra Raimondo: "O father, I see you do not know my wretched state. For I, a miserable woman, have received so many wonderful gifts from my Creator, but I am vile because anyone who had received such should be aflame and burn with the love of God and contempt for the present life, ceasing from their sins. Since I do not do this, what can I say about myself but that I am most ungrateful to my God and the ruin of all? If I did my duty, I would call them back by the food of God's word and influence them to act rightly by the example of a good life."

After this, Bartolomeo became her most ardent follower and champion, and frequently acted as the confessor for her

Division among the Franciscans

It seems odd, doesn't it, that the Franciscans would have objections to Catherine's goals and spiritual work? This is because the Franciscan Order had fallen on difficult times in Catherine's day, and there were great divisions between those friars who wanted to live most faithfully to Francis's teachings, and others who ruled the order and, in the process, lessened Francis's rules on personal and corporate poverty. No doubt, this Friar Lazzarino would have been part of the ruling order within the order, rather than a part of what were called the "Spirituals." The Spirituals, in contrast, would rather have been fools than churchmen. The ministers who followed Francis most closely in those early days were opposed to the ways that Francis's movement had fast become an order: *undertaking fundraising, building cathedrals, and devising intellectual systems that would endanger the Poverello's single-minded passion for firsthand experience. The Spirituals were soon excluded from the inner workings of the order for their staunch stand on these issues. After a decisive series of intra-order battles in the first two decades of the fourteenth century, Pope John XXII had declared the ideas of the Spirituals heretical, but their groups lived on in the hill towns and more remote areas of Italy. Many among them became Catherine's early supporters.*

and all of her spiritual companions. One day, a Franciscan friar by the name of Fra Lazzarion of Pisa followed Bartolomeo to Catherine. He was an eloquent and popular preacher, a man of considerable learning, but by no means an exemplary Franciscan as far as his vow of poverty was concerned. Lazzarino was lecturing on philosophy in Siena at this time, and Bartolomeo had come to know Lazzarino while Bartolomeo was himself lecturing occasionally on the *Sentences* of Peter Lombard. Lazzarino had heard of Catherine and was known to make fun of her in both public and private.

With a pretense of devotion but the intention of catching her in saying or doing something inappropriate, Lazzarino followed his acquaintance to her cell. Allow Bartolomeo himself to relate what happened next: "When we entered her holy cell, Fra Lazzarino sat down upon a stool. She seated herself at his feet upon the floor, while I took a seat on the opposite side. Both of them kept silence

46

for a while. After some time, Lazzarino began, 'I have heard such good reports of your holiness and your understanding of the scriptures that I have come in hopes of hearing something edifying for my soul.' She answered him, 'I am glad that you came, for I believe the Lord has sent you to teach me and to comfort my poor little soul. And so, for the love of Jesus Christ, I pray you deign to do.' The rest of the evening passed in conversation and soon, night was at hand. By the time Lazzarino went away, he took little account of her, deeming her to be a good woman, but not worthy of her great reputation."

The following night, Lazzarino rose to meditate on the lecture that he was to deliver the next morning and found himself overwhelmed with tears. In the morning, he forced himself to go to the schools and read his lecture perfunctorily, but left the room at once when he had finished. So he passed the day until, that evening, he began to think that he had unwittingly offended God. Then a voice spoke in his heart: "Have you so soon forgotten that, the day before, you scorned my faithful handmaid Catherine with so arrogant a mind?" Before the sun rose again, he left his room and hurried back to Catherine's house. Catherine herself, "knowing of the things that were being worked in this man by her Spouse," opened the door. He fell at her feet, and she implored him to rise. Entering the cell, he sat down humbly like she had done on the floor and after "a long and holy colloquy" asked her to adopt him as a son and to direct him in the way of God. "But when she said that he knew the way of God better, by means of his knowledge of holy scripture, he answered that he knew the rind but she tasted the very pith. Some time later, urged on by his earnest wishes, she answered: 'The way of salvation for your soul is in despising the pomp of the world and all its favor, casting away all money and superfluities, as you

47

**Anti-clericalism among
Catherine's Early Followers**

*There was plenty of anti-clericalism in
the church in Italy around 1350. Two
splinter groups of religious conserva-
tives, in particular, had run up against
popes and other priests, creating an
environment where religious fervor was
often experienced as contrary to the
needs and desires of the church. One
of these groups was the aforementioned
Spirituals, among the Franciscans.
The other was called the Flagellants.
These disorganized bands of spiritual
zealots first appeared on the scene in the
generation after St. Francis of Assisi,
about a century before St. Catherine.
They would scourge themselves pub-
licly, explaining to crowds of horrified
onlookers that they were practicing
penance demanded by God. The Black
Death of 1348 only heightened the
passion of these groups, and a year
later Pope Clement VI had to issue a
papal bull forbidding them from public
assembly.*

follow Christ crucified and your father, Blessed Francis, in naked-ness and humility."'

Fra Lazzarino seemed changed into another man. He gave away all that he had, even his books, except for a com-mentary on the Gospels that he needed for his sermons, "and really became a true poor man of Christ." He became a zealous champion of Catherine's cause, enduring much criticism from his own brothers. One of his fellow Franciscans tells us that he fled the society of the other friars to live in lonely hermitages, from which he would emerge at times to preach to the people, and that on these occasions his words were like flaming arrows to pierce the hearts of all who heard them.

CHAPTER FOUR
Pope Urban V

The abbot of St. Victor of Marseilles was in Florence, on his way to Naples on a mission from the pope to Queen Giovanna, when news reached him that Pope Innocent VI was dead. "I dare to say," he wrote upon hearing the news, "that if by God's grace I were to see a pope who would come back to Italy, to the true papal seat, and would battle the tyrants, I would be happy if I had to die the following day." When this fine abbot, Guillaume de Grimoard, returned to Marseilles at the end of October 1362, he was met by a message from the Sacred College informing him that (because of a deadlock in the conclave) he had been elected the next pope. He was crowned at Avignon under the title of Urban V.

He was fifty-three years old. Never having been a cardinal, he was untainted by the corruption of the Roman curia. A man of simple life, learned and devout, he hated pomp and luxury, simony and nepotism, and all the vices he saw around him.

Wars raged everywhere. France was at war with England, the emperor on the point of hostilities with the king of Hungary, who in his turn was assailing the Venetians. Italy was in a state of anarchy. Each peace, whether in France or in Italy, set loose fresh hordes of mercenaries who moved over the lands almost unchecked. In vain, Urban polished bull after bull, hurling anathemas at the armies and their leaders. In the latter part of 1365, the French commander Bertrand du Guesclin besieged the pope himself in Avignon, forcing him to pay an enormous ransom, and to absolve him and his followers from all censures. It was perhaps this humiliation that induced Pope Urban V to carry out his old resolution to return the papacy to Rome. The Spanish Franciscan, Peter of Aragon, came to Avignon with an impassioned dream of the reformation of the church, and Petrarch also made an eloquent appeal. The emperor was favorable to the idea, and in spite of the opposition of the king of France, Urban left Avignon on April 30, 1367.

On October 14, after extended stays at Corneto and Viterbo, Urban entered Rome in triumph, riding on a white mule, and was received with universal joy and acclamation. Armed mercenaries, both infantry and cavalry, surrounded the prelates and cardinals of the curia. Such was the martial entry of the vicar of the Prince of Peace; but the simple monk, Urban, who seemed to be the sovereign of the world, wept when he saw the desolation of the Sacred City, and threw himself in fervent prayer upon the ground at the tomb of the Apostle whose place he came to hold.

One week later, the pope and the emperor entered Rome together, Charles leading Urban V's mule on foot. This was the great event for which St. Bridget had waited so long in patience, but now that it had come, it brought her a personal disappointment. She had communicated her visions concerning the reformation of the church to Urban. She had written to the emperor, urging him to unite in this great work, and she now wrote again in the name of Christ, begging him to listen to her revelations and strive to make the divine justice and mercy feared and desired upon Earth. But Charles simply ignored her and Urban had no time, then, to attend to a woman's admonitions.

But much of Italy remained in near anarchy. In Catherine's Siena, the banished nobles held the fortresses in the *contado*, burned and foraged up to the gates of the city, and absolutely declined to come to terms with the government. And Perugia,

50

the third city of the papal states, was also still unsubdued, and only nominally subject to the church. In the October of 1369, Pope Urban received in Rome the emperor of the East, Johannes V Palaeologus, who came to ask for aid against the Turks. Thus the pope, in the space of a single year, had seen the successors of Charlemagne and Justinian alike at his feet—but still found his power defied by small hill town republics in Tuscany and Umbria.

In April 1370, Urban left Rome for the last time, returning to Viterbo, about sixty miles north of Rome. On May 22, an embassy from the Romans came to implore the pope to reconsider his decision. "The Holy Spirit led me to Rome," he answered. "Now it leads me away for the honor of the Church." Ill health and the evil influence of the French cardinals were probably the real explanations. The only plausible excuse that Urban could have offered was that his presence was needed in Avignon to make peace between France and England, who had renewed hostilities. On June 7, he made two cardinals, both of whom were soon to touch Catherine's life: Pierre d'Estaing and the bishop of Florence, Piero Corsini. He then bade the Romans farewell, promising to care for them as a father, urging them to remain at peace and not prevent his return or the coming of his successor. "We bear witness," he said, "that we and our brothers, the cardinals of the Holy Roman Church, have remained for three years with you in great quiet and consolation. And you, collectively and individually, have treated us and our Curia with reverence and kindness."

St. Bridget had traveled to Viterbo where the pope was. With her came a man of holy reputation whom we will meet again in connection with Catherine: the "hermit bishop," Alfonso da Vadaterra. Born of a Sienese father and a Spanish mother,

Alfonso had begun a brilliant ecclesiastical career as bishop of Jaen, but had renounced his bishopric, distributed his goods among the poor, and was now living at Rome as an Augustinian hermit. It was he who wrote Bridget's life, and apparently put the books of her *Revelations* into the form in which we now have them.

Urban received Bridget kindly, granted her the authorization of her rule, but refused to discuss the affairs of the Holy See. But soon afterward she left him, and he sent a messenger to her to ask what the divine will might be in these matters. The visionary spirit seized on Bridget, and she responded:

> Because of my prayer, he obtained the infusion of the Holy Spirit that he should go through Italy to Rome, for nothing else but to do justice and mercy, to strengthen the Catholic faith, to confirm peace, and to renovate the holy Church. As a mother leads her child to what place pleases her while she shows him her breasts, so did I lead Pope Urban by my prayer and the work of the Holy Spirit from Avignon to Rome, without any danger to his person. What has he done to me? Now he turns his back to me and intends to depart. . . . The devil draws him with worldly things [and] he is drawn, too, by the counsels of his carnal friends, who consider his pleasure and will more than the honor and will of God, or the profit and salvation of his soul. If he returns to the region where he was elected Pope, he will soon receive a stroke and gnash his teeth, his sight will be darkened and grow dim, and all the limbs of his body will tremble. . . . And he will render account before God of the things that he has done in the papal chair, and of the things that he has not done, but could have, to the honor of God.

This *Revelation* (number 4) was delivered by Bridget in person to the pope, in the presence of the young French cardinal Pierre Roger de Beaufort, but Urban went sadly on his way. On September 5, 1370, he sailed from Corneto, reaching France on September 16. Three months later, he died at Avignon in the house of his brother, away from the pomp of his office and dressed in a simple Benedictine habit. An ineffectual pope, Urban V was a faithful monk to the end. According to Bridget, in spite of his great fall, Urban's soul finds mercy at last because of his fidelity to his vows.

The year that Pope Urban V deserted Italy is the year of Catherine's entry into public life. On December 30, that young French cardinal, Pierre Roger de Beaufort, was elected to succeed Urban, and he took the name Gregory XI. The new pontiff, Gregory XI, was gentle, scholarly, sickly, well meaning, but also weak and irresolute. He was fickle and at times unexpectedly hard and obstinate. And he was soon to encounter the spiritual force of Catherine of Siena.

A Portrait of Two Popes
—Urban V and Gregory XI

Urban V (1362–70) and Gregory XI (1370–78) were both reforming popes. Urban ultimately failed to return the papacy to Rome, but most historians agree that Bridget and others were too harsh on him. His reform efforts on financial abuses and in the area of education were remarkable. Gregory XI carried on some of these efforts, as well as the attempt to return the papacy to Rome. After Urban V's death, Gregory XI urged canonization for his predecessor, but found little support. After his own death, an era of competing popes, an Italian in Rome and a Frenchman in Avignon, began.

CHAPTER FIVE
The Beginnings of Her Public Life

Catherine was then nearly twenty-four years old. A sixteenth-century historian once stated that Catherine had already written to a pope—Pope Urban V—by this time. But this is an error. Her time had not yet come to pass out of her hidden life into what a pope of the Renaissance called the "game of the world." Her entry into public affairs began in the months that intervened between Urban's flight from Italy and his death at Avignon.

All through the summer of 1370, Catherine's soul was overwhelmed with visions of divine mysteries. "To explain in our defective language what I saw," she said years later, "would seem to me like blaspheming the Lord or dishonoring him by my speech. Great is the distance between what the intellect apprehends, rapt and illumined and strengthened by God, and what can be expressed with words. They seem almost contradictory." When she prayed for purity of heart that she might worthily receive the blessed sacrament, it seemed to her that a flood of mingled blood and fire was poured down on her, for the mystical cleansing of her body and soul. And a day or two later, she believed that Christ had drawn her heart from her side and given her his own in exchange. "Don't you see, father," she said to Fra Tommaso della Fonte, "that I am no longer who I was, but that I am changed into another person?"

On another occasion while praying for this confessor and her other companions, she asked for a sign that her prayers were being heard. It was then that she felt the piercing of the palm of her outstretched hand, as though by an invisible nail of iron, and received the foretaste of the stigmata. The imprint of the five wounds of Christ's passion, albeit invisible on Catherine's body, were hers. She prayed earnestly that she would soon be delivered from the body that kept her from the full embraces of her spouse, and that, if this wasn't possible, she might meanwhile be at least united to him by partaking in the sufferings that he endured on Earth.

It was soon after this event, on a Sunday in the autumn of 1370, that a sort of mystical death fell upon Catherine—a trance of about four hours in duration—during which her friends thought she was dead. Fra Bartolomeo di Domenico tells us that he was preaching in San Domenico when the report came that Catherine had died. He rushed to her cell, and it was already so full of friars and women in tears that he could hardly enter. They told him that she had been dead for several hours.

Catherine felt that her heart had been broken by the force of Christ's love. She said, "So great was the fire of divine love and of the desire of uniting myself with him that, if my heart had been made of stone or iron, it would have been broken in the same manner." During this suspension of her bodily life, Catherine believed that she had really died and that her soul entered into eternity, tasted the blessedness of the vision of the Divine Essence, and saw heaven, purgatory, and hell. The *Legenda* reports her account:

> While my soul saw all of these things, the eternal Bridegroom said to me, "Do you see the great glory that some are deprived of, and the horrible torments that await them, who offend me? Return, then, and make known to them their errors, their danger, and loss. The salvation of many souls demands your return. No longer will you keep the way of life that you have kept; no longer will you have your cell for a home. You are to leave your own city for the sake of the

welfare of souls. I will be with you and guide you and bring you back again. I will give you speech and wisdom that no one will be able to withstand. I will lead you before pontiffs and rulers of the churches and all Christian people.

Soon afterward, Fra Bartolomeo arrived at her cell and Catherine gradually came back to life. But for days she could do nothing but cry for the sad state of her soul, which, having seen the angels and the face of her Creator, was sent down again to carnal imprisonment. Until her death, she believed that she had been truly dead and she couldn't speak of her vision without tears. This vision was the prelude to her public life—the mystical signification of her great and wonderful vocation.

Public Problems

From that time forward, Catherine's work was done openly in the eyes of the world. Her witness became the impetus for conversions and she gained many followers, many of them young and earnest men. That a young woman would be surrounded by men in this way, some of them as young as she was, gave food to cynical thoughts and slanderous tongues. The most bitter of the accusations for Catherine to bear came from a woman named Andrea, whom she was tending while dying slowly of cancer.

Who Was Brother Elias?
The Elias mentioned here was a historical figure who lived in the century before Catherine. He was two years older than Francis of Assisi, and one of his early, closest friends. Elias grew up in and around Assisi and knew Francis from their childhood. A shadow hangs over him in the narrative of the early Franciscan movement, as he appears to have had ulterior motives for sanctity from early on. Elias enjoyed power but lacked the creativity that marked most of the other early followers of Francis. He was elected minister-general of the order after Peter Catani, but his rule was controversial. He was seen as despotic to some, even essentially evil,

especially to those who rejected any changes made to Francis's original intentions. As Gardner mentions, Elias was famous for his love of luxury, in contrast to his spiritual father. It was largely due to Elias's influence that the great basilica for St. Francis was built in Assisi, after the saint's death. Pope Gregory IX dismissed Elias in 1239 for wrongdoing, and one year later, Elias joined Emperor Frederick II, a violent enemy of the church, as an advisor. After a decade of serving Frederick II (whose mercenaries were famously repelled by St. Clare in their attempt to besiege San Damiano), Elias repented his sins to a priest and the excommunication placed on him was lifted. He died in 1253.

Andrea accused Catherine to the prioress and sisters of the Mantellate as guilty of unchastity. At the first pang of this lying accusation, Catherine prayed to God with tears, asking for him to prove her innocence, but he responded that she must choose between a crown of pearls and the crown of thorns, and so she eagerly accepted the latter.

It was probably about this time that a last attempt was made from the religious people of Siena to hinder Catherine's work. It came from two men who were respected as religious leaders in the city. One was Fra Gabriele da Volterra, a Franciscan and minister of the province and also a Master of Sacred Theology with a great reputation for learning and preaching. Fra Gabriele was a sort of Brother Elias who lived sumptuously in the convent of San Francesco like a great prelate.

The other was a friar of the order of Augustinian hermits, Fra Giovanni Tantucci (usually known as Giovanni Terzo in order to distinguish him from two other Brother Johns in his convent). He was also a Master of Sacred Theology, and had been to England, where he had taken his doctor's degree at the University of Cambridge.

These two friars began to murmur against Catherine, in orthodox pharisaical fashion, saying that she was an ignorant woman who was seducing simple people with false expositions of holy scripture. They resolved to make her recognize her errors and came to visit her one day with two other companions. A number of men and women were with Catherine when they arrived, and Francesco Malavolti tells the tale of what happened:

> While we were listening to the wonderful words of the holy virgin, she suddenly broke off in her speech and her countenance was glowing. She raised her eyes to heaven and said, "Blessed be you, sweet and eternal Bridegroom, who finds so many new ways and paths by which to draw souls to yourself." We were all attention, considering what she had done, for her motions and words were full of mystery and without any obvious cause. Then, the father Fra Tommaso, her confessor, said to her: "Tell me, what is the meaning of what you have just done? What do you mean?" And she answered, "Father, you will soon see two great fish caught in the nets." She said no more. And while we were still in suspense and expecting some resolution to the affair, one of Catherine's companions who lived in the house with her, said: "Mother, there are two men here with their companions, wishing to see you."

As Catherine was going to meet them, the two came into the room. They sat down and "like two furious lions" the Franciscan and Augustinian began to ply her with the most difficult theological questions, hoping to confuse her before her friends and disciples. Francesco Malavolti again recounts:

> But the Holy Spirit granted her great wisdom and fortitude. Aflame with divine zeal, Catherine rebuked their inflated and useless science, showing them that they had set their hearts on the praises of others, and spoke so winningly of the love

59

of Christ that the two were converted. Master Gabriele was living in such pomp that in his convent he had made himself one cell out of three, and furnished it so sumptuously that it would have been excessive for a cardinal. Taking his keys from his girdle, he said before us all: "Will someone here go and distribute and give away all that I have in my cell, for the love of God? Leave me nothing but my breviary." Gabriele himself left shortly afterwards and went to Santa Croce in Florence, and there he began to serve the friars in the refectory and in other acts of humility, although he was still the minister of the province. Master Giovanni also gave away all that he had, keeping only his breviary, and became one of Catherine's immediate followers, accompanying her in her travels until her death. In fact, he was one of the three confessors who were deputed by the pope to hear confessions of those who were converted by her.

Through Master Giovanni Tantucci, Catherine also came into contact with the hermits of Lecceto. The convent of San Salvatore di Lecceto was the head house in Tuscany of the Augustinian hermits, "a blessed place" writes one seventeenth-century historian, "in which the Most High chose to work so many wonders." It lies a few miles west of Siena in what remains of a once glorious forest. During the Middle Ages, wonderful legends had lingered about the convent and forest. Miraculous waters had gushed out of the arid soil; the stones had taken mystical colors in commemoration of Christ; and the flowers of the forest had wonderful healing properties, "all evident signs that here flourished a continual spring of Paradise."

The great days of the convent, however, were a thing of the past. And there were evidently some opposed to Catherine living there. William Flete was an Englishman from Cambridge who had settled down among the hermits at Lecceto, led there, perhaps, by his acquaintance Giovanni Tantucci. In Catherine's circles these two scholars were usually spoken of by their academic degrees: Giovanni being the "Master," and William the "Bachelor." William appears to have led a life more austere than his rule asked of him, devoting himself to penance and study, avoiding all conversation with outsiders, and associating very little with the other friars. It is clear from one of Catherine's letters to him that she felt he was devoted to mortification for its own sake. There are those, she tells William, "who have set their desire more in mortifying the body than in slaying their own will. They are fed at the table of penance and are perfect, but if they haven't a great humility and don't learn to judge according to the will of God rather than that of men, then they often ruin their perfection by making themselves judges of those on the same road as they.

"People who are like this always wish to choose the time and place when they will encounter tribulations from the world and assaults from the devil. And thus they fall into pain and weariness and become unbearable to themselves, further marring their perfection. The taint of pride lies in this, but they do not perceive it. But if one such as this were truly humble and not

Direct and Indirect Knowledge of God

Catherine is quoted in the Legenda *as saying that her knowledge of God came directly from God, and as we know, she was uneducated in any formal sense. Still, as one scholar explains: "In reading her works we cannot help sensing the presence of various sources, such as Thomas Aquinas or Augustine and, most frequently, Holy Scripture. How can their presence be accounted for? The liturgy and the sermons that Catherine heard at St. Dominic's are no doubt chiefly responsible for her knowledge of texts which she certainly did not read. Conversation with her followers, which included distinguished lay members, Dominicans and other religious, must not be undervalued" (Cavallini, 17).*

61

presumptuous, he would surely see that the first sweet Truth gives time, place, consolation, and tribulation according to how we need these things for our salvation, and to complete in the soul the perfection for which she is chosen. And he would see that it gives everything for love, and therefore with love."

A little while later, we find Catherine urging William Flete, as well as his hermit companion, not to allow their love of solitude to draw them away from their duties:

"I tell you, not only should you say Mass in the convent sometimes during the week when the prior wishes it, but I want you to say it every day, if you see that he wishes it. I want us not to attend only to our own consolations, but we must also care and have compassion for the labors of our neighbors. If you didn't do this it would be a very great fault."

CHAPTER SIX
From the Cell to the World

I'll seek my love straightaway
Over yon hills, down where yon streamlets flow.
To pluck no flowers I'll stay;
No fear of beasts I'll know;
Past mighty men, o'er frontier-grounds I'll go.
—ST. JOHN OF THE CROSS

These were stormy days for Siena. Plots were constant, and the government retaliated with torture and executions. At the beginning of 1371, a conspiracy was discovered and two culprits were sentenced to be *attanagliati*, that is, torn by hot pincers while on a cart meandering through the city to the place of execution. Catherine was in the house of Alessa when the dreadful pageant passed through the street below. At her prayers, the horrible shrieks and despairing blasphemies of the condemned men were hushed and a vision of Christ came to meet them at the gate of the city. "They went to death as joyously as though they were invited to a banquet," the *Legenda* records.

In July of the same year, a secret association of wool carders, a union that had been forbidden to assemble, shook the whole fabric of the state for a while. For several days the insurgents held the city at their mercy and compelled the government to put seven of their own into the Signoria (literally, "Lord"), or governing party. This was followed by a counterconspiracy, and then a massacre in the Costa d'Ovile on July 30, where the counter-rising was crushed.

Almost immediately after leaving the seclusion of her father's house, we find Catherine in touch with the politics of her native

63

city, and with the great questions that were agitating the whole church. Not only are the spears and swords of contending factions lowered before her as she passes along the streets of Siena, but the princes and potentates of Italy seem to realize instantly that a new spiritual power has arisen in the land. From Avignon, the pope himself seemed to gladly know that there were secrets Christ had hidden from him, but not from the simple maiden.

This was due, in part, to the effect produced upon Pope Gregory XI's mind by the revelations of St. Bridget. From the beginning of his pontificate, the Swedish princess had exhorted him to repair the scandal caused by the defection of his predecessor. In a vision she heard the voice of the Blessed Virgin, promising that if Gregory would restore the papal chair to Rome and reform the church, her prayers would flood his soul with spiritual joy from her divine Son. If not, the Blessed Virgin communicated to Bridget, Gregory would surely feel the rod of Christ's indignation, his life would be cut short, and he would be summoned to judgment. Bridget wrote to ask the pope to come to Italy by the beginning of the following April (presumably 1372) at the latest, if he would like to have the Blessed Virgin as a mother and escape the judgments of God.

At her bidding, the hermit-bishop Alfonso of Jaen brought this letter to Perugia and entrusted it to the count of Nola for transmission to the pope. A copy was shown to the sinister Gerard du Puy, abbot of Marmoutier, and then destroyed.

There was one significant passage in the revelation that was reserved for Gregory alone. "Unless the Pope," said Bridget to Alfonso (speaking in the person of the Blessed Virgin), "comes to Italy at the time and in the year appointed, the lands of the Church, that are now united under his sway and obedience, will be divided in the hands of his enemies. To augment the tribulation of the Pope, he will not only hear but will see that what I say is true. These words that I now say to you are not yet to be told or written to Abbot Marmoutier, for the seed is hidden in the earth until it fructifies in ears of corn." This prophecy was soon fulfilled to the letter.

Gregory XI, who had asked the abbot to demand an explanation for the first revelation, offered no response to the second. And Bridget, seeing no hope of the pope's returning, started for the Holy Land in the autumn of 1371 accompanied by Alfonso and a few others.

On July 23, 1373, St. Bridget died in Rome. Her daughter Catherine took the body to Sweden and then returned to Rome, awaiting the coming of the pope that her mother had promised. Petrarch died in the following year. And in the meanwhile, the other Catherine had taken up the work that the Italian poet and the Swedish princess had left incomplete, beginning with the two formidable prelates of the Church Militant who were meeting over Bridget's revelations: Cardinal Pietro d'Estaing and Gerard du Puy, the abbot of Marmoutier and nephew to Gregory XI.

First Letters Dealing with Political Matters

Cardinal d'Estaing was an upright man, but had proven to be a stern and unpopular ruler of Perugia. At the end of 1371, Pope Gregory XI appointed him to the legation of Bologna, succeeding Cardinal Anglicus Grimoard. The following January, d'Estaing made a pompous triumphal entry into Bologna and was seen by the inhabitants to be a champion of freedom against the fearsome soldier and lord of Milan, Bernabo Visconti. "Cardinal d'Estaing was reputed a very great and upright man," writes one chronicler, "and they say that he had great legatorial powers, and more authority from the Pope than had ever been given to another representative of the Church." That August, the bishop of Cavaillon, Philippe de Cabassoles, died, and was succeeded by the abbot of Marmoutier (who had come to Italy in the preceding year as treasurer general of the church). Gerard du Puy thus became the governor of Perugia, with the title of vicar apostolic.

Now begins the series of Catherine's correspondences with these two men. Among the first of them that we can date with any certainty are the two to Cardinal d'Estaing. They are, as it were, the frontispiece to the whole mystical volume of her epistles. They give us the essence of her spiritualized political doctrine. Italy is the prologue, peace the epilogue. Love of charity is the rule; self-love and servile fear are the enemies to be overthrown. The philosophy that she learned from the Prince of Peace in her cell is applied to the political state of the church and the world. Already we see her soul overwhelmed by the impassioned dream of a reformation of the church down to its very foundations—*infino alle fondamenta*, to use her own words—that is soon to lead her across the Alps, as ambassador of Christ as well as of Florence, to reconcile the pope with Italy and bring him back to Rome.

It was early in 1372 that Catherine first addressed a letter to Cardinal d'Estaing, opening with a play on the words *legato* and *Legato*, which is impossible to render into English. "Dearest and reverend father in Christ sweet Jesus," she begins, "I, Catherine, servant and slave of the servants of Jesus Christ, write to you in his precious blood with the desire of seeing you bound in the bond of charity even as you have been made Legate in Italy, as I have heard, and at which I have been singularly delighted, considering that by this you will be able to do much for the honor of God and the Church. But you know that we can do no work of grace in ourselves, or for our neighbor, without love. Love is the sweet and holy bond that binds the soul with her Creator; it binds God in man and man in God. This inestimable love kept God and Man fastened and nailed upon the wood of the most holy cross." She continues, saying that it is love or charity alone that unites the separated, makes war to cease, gives patience and perseverance, and that it is founded on the living rock of Christ. Bound in this love, she urges the representative of the supreme pontiff to follow in the footsteps of Christ:

> I ask you, then, to follow Christ's footsteps with manly heart and ready zeal, never turning aside by reason of either pain or pleasure, but persevering to the end in every work that you undertake to do for Christ crucified. Strive to extirpate the iniquities and miseries of the world. Do your utmost to find a remedy for all of this. I am certain that, if you are bound in the sweet bond of love, you will use your legation that you have received from the Vicar of Christ in this way.

Catherine follows this up with a second letter, "with desire of seeing you a virile and brave man, so that you may manfully serve the Spouse of Christ, using both spiritual and temporal means for God's honor, as this Spouse needs in these necessary times." She tells him to open the eyes of his understanding, to beware of servile fear (a favorite doctrine of Catherine's, which we find her repeating again and again in almost the same words), and to look on the Lamb who sought only the honor of the Father, and feared nothing. "We are the scholars," she writes, "who have been sent to this sweet and gentle school." And the time has come to put these lessons into practice. She continues:

Strive manfully, to the utmost of your power, to bring about peace and union to the whole country. And if, for this holy work, it proves necessary to give your life, you should give it a thousand times over. Where all faithful Christians should be preparing to make war upon the infidels, false Christians are waging it against each other, and the demons are rejoicing because they see what they want to see. I am certain that you will do this manfully, if you are clothed with the new man, Christ Jesus, and stripped of the old. Peace, peace, peace! Dearest father, make the Holy Father consider the loss of souls more than that of cities; for God demands souls more than cities.

Her Emasculating Words

How difficult it must have been for a powerful man of the fourteenth century to hear a woman, one of his contemporaries, even someone of Catherine's growing stature, urge him to be more "manful" and "virile." Catherine learned this way of talking to powerful men from Bridget of Sweden before her. Catherine also saw a precedent in Bridget for hearing God "speak" to her heart about corrupt ecclesiastics. Throughout her Liber Celestis (Book of Visions), *God reveals secret corruption to Bridget. In one instance, God gives her a vision of "a certain cleric whom she knew well . . . a man who was very learned in divinity, but was nevertheless full of the Devil's own deceit and wickedness." At another time, about another priest, Bridget heard Christ say to her, "That jangling cleric is too proud of his learning to want me. But I*

Meanwhile, Gerard du Puy, the abbot of Marmoutier, was one of the worst of those rapacious wolves in sheep's clothing to whom the popes of Avignon had entrusted their flocks. While Cardinal d'Estaing was vigorously pursuing reforms and fighting the oppressions of Bernabo Visconti without oppressing the subjects of the church, du Puy was governing Perugia with detestable tyranny. He was building two great fortresses connected by a large covered way supported by arches, over which his troops could pass back and forth. He ground the people down with taxes, excluded all the citizens

68

from his counsels, and ruled the province with corrupt notaries and foreign captains. He connived at the most outrageous offences committed by his officials, and protests from the injured parties he would answer with cynicism. Nevertheless, this detestable monk had been the intermediary between the pope and St. Bridget, and now, probably immediately after Bridget's death in 1373, he appealed to Catherine.

We don't know how he appealed to Catherine, or whether she was aware of the character of the monk with whom she was

shall give him a clout and he will really know that I am God." The narrative continues: "And shortly after that he died of the palsy" (Bridget, 147, 149).

By Catherine's day, there was precedent for powerful religious women who had spiritual influence over the most powerful religious men. One thinks of St. Brigid of Ireland, as well, as one of Catherine's predecessors. Like St. Patrick, Brigid battled the pagan traditions of the druids while working to establish Christianity in Ireland. She died in the early 520s and tradition has her buried in Downpatrick, one of the towns that claims to be the burial place of St. Patrick. A ninth-century life of Brigid called the Bethu Brigte suggests that the saint held "episcopal ordination," the spiritual orders equivalent to a bishop.

now dealing, but her answer is extant and is one of the most striking of her political letters. To this wicked man, too, she writes in the precious blood of God, "with desire of seeing you a true priest and a member bound in the body of holy Church."

The first part of the letter is an impassioned hymn to love. "This is the way of Christ crucified, who will always give us the light of peace." She then describes that there are two things in particular that are disfiguring the church and must be taken away: nepotism, "excessive tenderness and solicitude for kinsmen," and leniency in dealing with wickedness in clergy. "Christ especially hates three perverse sins: impurity, avarice, and the puffed-up pride that reigns in some of the clergy, who attend to pleasures and riches. They see the demons carrying off

69

the souls of their congregations, and they don't care, because they have become wolves and sellers of divine grace."

She advises the influential but wayward abbot: "You must labor together with the Holy Father, to the utmost of your power, in removing the wolves and incarnate demons of pastors who do little but eat and keep their palaces. What Christ acquired on the wood of the Cross has been spent on harlots! I pray that, even if you die for it, you will tell the Holy Father to find a remedy for these iniquities. For virtue is the thing that makes a man noble and pleasing to God."

1373, A Dark Time

The year 1373 was marked by both dissensions and homicides, especially among the religious and the clergy. One Sienese chronicler tells us that the Augustinian friars murdered their provincial at Sant'Antonio; that the Friars Minor in Assisi fought with knives and fourteen were killed; and at Siena a young friar in San Domenico killed another. Every convent was divided against itself and the same thing was going on outside the convents. Every part of the state was divided by plotting and petty treasons. "And so the world is one darkness," concluded the chronicler.

A new senator of Siena, Count Mogliano from the Marches, was attempting to restore order by impartial executions of noble and plebian criminals alike, but the only result was a series of riots during which his own life, and that of his family, was threatened.

Three of Catherine's letters show the impressions of these events. For example, she wrote to Pietro, the priest of Semignano, who was feuding with another priest and apparently also leading a scandalous life in other respects. She sets before his eyes the dignity of the priesthood that he is violating with his impurity and his hatred, and threatens him with the judgments of God. "What a scandal it is to see two priests hate each other! It is a great miracle that God does not command the earth to swallow both of you up. Come then, while you are still able to receive mercy; hurry to Christ crucified, who will receive you gently."

And to the wife of the new senator, who had written to her in terror after a mob assailed her husband, Catherine replied that the woman had "no faith or hope except in the prayers of the servants of God," and she sent words of gentle comfort and a reminder that not a leaf can fall from the tree without the permission and will of God.

In northern Italy, as we have mentioned, Cardinal d'Estaing was strenuously fighting against Visconti. "He made more war on the lords of Milan than any other legate had done," remarks one chronicler in Bologna. But the Tuscan republics wavered between Bernabo Visconti and the pope. At the beginning of November 1373, an ambassador from Bernabo came to Siena. While in Siena, he sought a meeting with Catherine in the name of Bernabo and his ambitious wife, Beatrice della Scala (possibly with the idea of convincing her of their good intentions). If this was his purpose, the ambassador was manifestly unsuccessful.

71

Catherine promptly dictated to her secretaries the two long letters to Bernabo and Beatrice that we still possess. Unfortunately, the passages at the end of the letters, in which she directly answers their requests or questions, were regarded by her contemporaries as of only ephemeral interest, and so were not preserved. But reading between the lines, we gather that Bernabo, the tyrant of Milan and her clergy, had tried to represent himself to Catherine as a kind of scourge of God, divinely ordained to punish the iniquities of religion. To this despot, Catherine expounds the law of love as shown in the mystery of redemption. She speaks of the vanity of all earthly lordship, which may pass away at any moment, in comparison with the lordship of the city of the soul in which God rests, and which is impregnable. But in order to regain this spiritual freedom, one must be washed in the blood of Christ; this blood is kept in the body of the church, to be administered by the hands of Christ's clergy; and we cannot partake of it except through them. "I tell you, dear father, and brother in Christ sweet Jesus, that God doesn't wish you or anyone else to make yourself the executioner of his ministers. For he has reserved this to himself, and committed it to the pope. And if the pope does not do what he should, we must humbly await the punishment and chastisement of the Supreme Judge, God eternal, even if our possessions are taken from us by these men. I pray you, in the name of Christ, concern yourself no more with this. Keep your own cities in peace; punish your own subjects when they do wrong; but never touch those who are the ministers of the glorious and precious blood."

She then advised: Bernabo should become a faithful son of the church. "What amends will you need to make for the time that you have been outside?" she rhetorically asks. "It seems to me that a time is coming in which we will be able to make gracious amends, for as you have been at war with your father, now I invite you to true and perfect peace with that father, and to war upon the infidels, preparing to give your body and life for Christ crucified. I wish you to be the first to invite and urge the Holy Father to hurry, for it is a great shame and disgrace to Christians that infidels possess what is rightly ours."

To Beatrice, whose pride and avarice were infamous throughout Italy, Catherine writes "with desire of seeing you clothed in the robe of ardent charity, so that you will be an instrument in reconciling your husband with Christ sweet Jesus and with his pope, Christ on earth." From a letter addressed to Catherine by Elizabeth of Bavaria, the wife of Bernabo's son Marco (Petrarch's godson), we find that Catherine had thoughts of coming in person to Milan at this time. Elizabeth expresses her deep disappointment at hearing that the saint has changed her plans, and humbly commends her husband and little four-year-old daughter, Anna, to her prayers.

With these political letters, Catherine entered into the national life of her country. The lords of Italy and the prelates of the church had learned by now that her words had a power not their own. And either party was prepared and willing to make use of those words for their own ends and advantage.

In letters to the Cardinal of Bologna and his Milanese adversary alike, Catherine again refers to the Crusades. From the

Catherine and the Crusades
By this point in the life of Catherine, we have seen more than one occasion when she urged temporal leaders to use their power, not to lord it over others or fight in the factions of the church, but to crusade against the "infidels," meaning, people of other faiths. In so doing, she was echoing the urges of Pope Gregory XI and most of the other religious leaders of her time. However, by Catherine's birth, the epoch of European crusading to the Holy Land had long ended; the First Crusade had begun in 1095, and the Ninth, and last, took place in 1271–72.

beginning of his pontificate, Gregory XI had urged the power of Christendom to make peace among themselves and turn their arms against the Turks and Saracens. In particular, he had urged King Louis of Hungary to be a defender of the faith and use the great power that God had given him "for the defense of God's people whom he has redeemed by the shedding of his most precious blood, and so, a perishable earthly kingdom may pass to an eternal one." At the beginning of 1373, Gregory proclaimed the Crusade. St. Bridget, as we saw, had raised a prophetic voice against this scheme, as one that merely afforded an excuse to the pope for neglecting his more immediate duty, and an opportunity for the mercenary soldiers to plunder and ravage on a more extensive scale than was possible in Christendom. But Catherine, on the contrary, was enthusiastically supportive of the papal announcement.

Catherine saw in the proposed Crusade the possible liberation of the sepulcher of Christ and the deliverance of Italy from these armed pests that, like the eagle upon Prometheus, were feeding upon her organs. Visions passed before her eyes of crowds of martyrs offering up their blood for the redemption of the Holy Land, of men who had previously fought only for money, now putting on the sign of the cross and using their strength and ardor to battle for the faith.

But the cloud was already gathering on the horizon that would abort the pope's plans and make even Catherine's pleadings of no avail. Early in the following year (1374), the pope recalled Cardinal d'Estaing and appointed Guillaume de Noellet to take his place as papal legate in Italy and governor of Bologna. The new legate entered Bologna on March 15: "He came through Tuscany and when he arrived at Florence the Florentines showed him great honor. But here we did not welcome him as we had done the others, because this novelty of changing cardinal was too frequent. May God send us one who will be good for this city," wrote one Bolognese chronicler. It was a most unfortunate choice. Cardinal de Noellet was a tyrannical and incompetent French prelate of the usual type furnished by Avignon. He and his colleague, the abbot of Perugia, would quickly drive their Italian subjects to desperation.

This was a dismal year for all of Italy, and especially for Catherine's native city. "In Siena," writes one of her chroniclers at the opening of the year, "there was pestilence, war, and great scarcity, so that the bushel of grain was worth two golden florins."

In the spring, a fierce war broke out on a small scale in the Sienese *contado*. One of the Salimbeni had seized Perolla, a castle of Maremma, bordering the province of Siena, and hurled the daughter of its late lord down from the battlements. Secure in this stronghold, the Salimbeni—Andrea di Niccolo—gathered bandits and mercenaries around him, murdered and plundered all through the Maremma region, and began to levy blackmail up to the very gates of Siena itself. With aid from the Florentines, the Sienese gathered a large army, with the help of their senator, and forced these bandits to surrender on April 23. The senator returned to Siena with twenty-nine prisoners, including Andrea himself, and sixteen were executed. But the senator, either by reasons of friendship or for fear of the Salimbeni, did not do justice on the chief offender, Andrea. Upon this the populace armed and assailed the palace, demanding justice with threats. One of the mob, Noccio di Vanni, a saddler by trade, became their leader and, breaking into the palace, took his seat on the bench as judge and condemned Andrea to instant execution. He was promptly beheaded.

Indignant at the affront upon their house, the Salimbeni rose up in arms throughout the *contado*. They seized various areas of

the county, ravaged the hills and valleys, making war throughout the area, defying the forces of the Republic. From Perugia,
the abbot of Marmoutier sent agents to both parties, offering
to mediate, but was suspected (with good reason) of having a
secret understanding with the Salimbeni.

This frightful scourge happened throughout the month of
May, ravaging Tuscany all through the summer until September,
spreading through northern and central Italy, and even across
the Alps. While attacking all ages and classes, the mortality was
particularly terrible among the children. And the black shadow
of famine dogged its footsteps. There was a scarcity of everything, including bread, wine, meat, and oil. In the Tuscan cities,
the government collected all the materials that could be made
into bread and doled it out by ticket, but even so, there was not
enough to go around. The death carts went from street to street,
gathering up the dead; the priests, who tended the dying and
buried the victims, often shared their fate.

It was during this time that Catherine first left the territory
of her native city. Affected by the conflicting reports that had
reached his ears, the general of her order, Fra Elias of Toulouse,
summoned her to attend the chapter-general that met in Florence
in May. An anonymous Florentine contemporary paints the scene:
"There came to Florence in the month of May 1374, when the
chapter of the Friars Preachers was held, one wearing the habit of
the sisters of penance of St. Dominic, who was called Caterina di
Giacomo di Benincasa of Siena. She was twenty-seven years old
and deemed to be a great servant of God. With her she had three
other women, dressed in habits. Hearing of her fame, I managed to
see her and to gain her friendship in such a way that she often came
here into my house." We have no clue as to the identity of this
writer, or any record elsewhere of this first visit of Catherine to the

great city that was soon to be in the midst of such political turmoil.

The pestilence was already in Florence when Catherine was there, but the devastation was on a less dreadful scale than among the Sienese. Out of a population of sixty thousand, about seven thousand Florentines perished, and although we don't have the exact figures, the mortality rate in Siena appears to have been much higher. Catherine left Florence on June 29 and returned to her mother's house in Siena to find the pestilence raging, reminding all of the horrors of 1348.

Catherine's Family Home

"*The steep Via Benincasa—once the Via de'Tintori—leads up from Fontebranda into the town. . . . A few houses up the street, on the left, is a graceful building in the style of the early Renaissance, which now occupies the site of the house of Giacomo Benincasa: the Oratorio di Santa Caterina in Fontebranda. 'Many from beyond the mountains,' so runs an entry in the* Libro dei decreti de Concistoro *at the time when Catherine's canonization was in progress in Rome, 'French, Venetians, Romans and of other nations who have come to your city, have with great diligence asked for the house where dwelt in your city the blessed Catherine of Siena; and they have gone to it with great reverence and devotion, kneeling down in many places and kissing the walls and the door.'*" (Gardner, 191)

Catherine's and Raimondo's Work During the Crisis

Two of Catherine's brothers, Bartolomeo and Stefano, her sister Lisa, and eight of her nephews and nieces died. With her own hands, Catherine prepared the bodies for burial, saying over each of them: "This one, at least, I shall not lose." Her renown spread in these tumultuous times. With companions, she passed through the streets of the city, seeking out the most infected districts, entering the houses and hospitals, tending the sick and comforting the dying. They

The House of St. Catherine

prepared the bodies of the dead, many of whom she is said to have buried with her own hands. Several of them, including the hermit Fra Santi, and the priest of the Casa della Misericordia, gained so much strength from her healing attention that they rose up and followed her to give service to others.

Foremost among her fellow workers was the noble Dominican friar who soon became her spiritual director and afterward her first biographer, Fra Raimondo. It was he whom Catherine called, in her last letter, "father and son given to me by sweet Mother Mary." A man of aristocratic birth, Raimondo had been called in his youth to the Dominican Order in a way that he vaguely refers to

Hill Towns in Siena
Gardner has mentioned several of the hill towns of Tuscany thus far. The hill towns of Tuscany and nearby Umbria were the breeding ground for many of the Italian saints of the Middle Ages, and they have been rhapsodized by mystics and poets ever since those days. Siena itself is a hill town, obviously made famous by St. Catherine. One hundred kilometers away, Assisi was the hill town made famous by Sts. Francis and Clare in the century before St. Catherine. Montepulciano, meanwhile, is about seventy kilometers southeast of Siena, and stands about two thousand feet above sea level. As we will see below, Catherine makes a special trip to this hill town, which was associated with St. Agnes (1268–1317), who founded the convent of Dominican nuns mentioned below. After her death, it is said that St. Agnes's body refused to decompose and instead emitted a perfume.

as miraculous. He rapidly became a person of importance among the friars. He became prior of the Minerva at Rome in 1367, and shortly afterward was made director of the convent of Dominican nuns of Santa Agnes at Montepulciano. He spent two years there, and at the nuns' request, he wrote a life of their blessed patroness. Then Raimondo was sent to San Domenico at Siena as lector or professor of theology, and there he almost immediately took up Catherine's cause, arguing that she should never be hindered from communicating as often as she pleased. To Raimondo, Catherine found that she could open her heart in ways that were not possible with other men, and with the cordial and humble assent of Fra Tommaso, Fra Raimondo now took his place as her primary confessor and spiritual director.

Many other priests and religious men and women, like those among the laity who could afford it, had deserted the city. Fra Filippo tells a striking story of one of these, a moneylender and oppressor of the poor who converted all he had into ready money and fled to Massa when the pestilence first began. There he waited until he heard that it had abated. When he returned to the city, while drinking and laughing with his friends, he began to boast that he had jockeyed God. "And raising his eyes, he cried out at the top of his voice, 'You thought you would catch me, but you didn't!' But no sooner had he said this, than he said another in a lower tone: 'Woe is me. You did indeed get me, and now I feel the swelling!'" As the story goes, he straightaway went back to his house and died.

Worn out by her labors during the pestilence, Catherine herself fell dangerously ill on the Feast of the Assumption in 1374. With joy, she prayed for her death. But the Virgin Mary showed her all the souls whom, if her life was prolonged, she would guide toward eternal life—and she lived.

Catherine also believed that it was revealed to her that in paradise she would be the special companion of Agnes of Montepulciano. She felt a keen desire to visit that town, and after her recovery, traveled there together with Fra Raimondo and another of her confessors. Painter Girolamo del Pacchia's masterpiece still preserves the legend of how, as Catherine bent down over Agnes's incorrupt body to kiss her feet, one of them raised itself to meet her lips. The painter has united this with a similar episode that is said to have occurred a little later, when Catherine returned to Montepulciano. On this latter occasion, accompanied by her sister-in-law Lisa (who had returned to Siena after her husband's death and taken the habit of the Mantellate), Catherine laid her face on the silk that covered Agnes's dead face and, "Lisa and the others, lifting up their eyes, saw a very white and minute manna, like rain, descending from on high in such great abundance that it covered the body of Agnes and the virgin Catherine."

It was during that first stay in Montepulciano that Fra Raimondo's last doubts were dispelled concerning the divine origin of Catherine's works and revelations. Up until then, Raimondo's mind was unsure, "for I remembered that it was now the time of the third beast with the leopard's skin, signifying hypocrisy, and in my life I had met with hypocrites, especially young women, who are more easily and readily seduced by the Enemy, as is demonstrated in the case of our first Mother." But on that trip, Raimondo obtained a mental vision of his own sins with Catherine's help that was so clear, and a contrition so overwhelming, that he was convinced that he could not go on with anything but the grace of the Holy Spirit. A little later, when he again doubted the truth of what she was revealing to him, he saw her face transformed into the face of Christ and experienced a wonderful illumination concerning the matter of which she spoke.

Nevertheless, the good father was still not always able to follow Catherine's more ethereal flights. He confesses this with a measure of humor. On one occasion, when she was discoursing at great length on the divine mysteries, he fell asleep: "But she was all absorbed in God as she spoke, and went on with her discourse for a long time before she noticed that I was asleep. At last she noticed it and then woke me up by saying with a loud voice, 'Ah, why do you lose your soul's profit by sleeping? Am I talking about God to a wall or to you?'"

CHAPTER SEVEN
Her Influence Grows

Catherine was not always in Siena at this time of her life. Other cities in Tuscany were asking for her spiritual healing, and her great political work had begun. It was probably in the second half of 1374 that St. Bridget's confessor, the hermit-bishop Alfonso da Vadaterra, returned to Italy from Avignon. He came to Siena and sought a meeting with Catherine in the name of the pope, from whom he brought her the apostolic benediction, to enlist her spiritual influence for the papal intentions. "The Pope," writes Catherine in a letter to two of her friars, "has sent here one of his vicars—the spiritual father of that countess who died in Rome. It is he who renounced the bishopric for love of virtue, and he came to me in the name of the Holy Father, asking me to offer special prayers for him and for the Church. For a sign he brought me the holy indulgence. Rejoice then and be glad, for the Holy Father has begun to pay attention to the honor of God and of holy Church. I have written him a letter asking him to allow us to be persecuted for God's sake. Pray to the supreme eternal Truth that, if it is best, he may give us the mercy to give our lives for him." To Alfonso it must have seemed that the spirit of his dead friend lived again in the Sienese maiden, and he began to associate himself with her spiritual fellowship.

Friars had spread Catherine's fame throughout Pisa, and she began to receive invitations to visit there, including one from Piero Gambacorti, the ruler of the Pisan Republic. Her answer to Gambacorti is extant; she admonishes him to detach himself from the delights of the world and to keep his eyes fixed on divine justice in his governing. At the end, she excuses herself from coming on the grounds of her bad health and the risk of causing a scandal—relations then being strained between the Pisan and Sienese people.

Nevertheless, in early 1375, Catherine believed herself to have received a divine command to delay no longer, and she set out for Pisa. She was accompanied by Alessa, Lisa, Cecca, and also her mother, Monna Lapa, who did not want to be apart from her daughter. Also traveling with Catherine were Fra Raimondo, Fra Tommaso della Fonte, and Fra Bartolomeo, to hear the confessions of those whom she would convert to God. This little band received a royal reception at Pisa, met by Piero Gambacorti himself, and also by the archbishop and other religious and political notables. They were entertained and lodged in the house of one of Pisa's leading citizens, a house that stood on the Arno near the little chapel of Santa Cristina. Here, the same wonders were enacted as had been done in Siena: the sick were healed, people were brought to repentance. "I saw her speak to certain sinners," wrote Giovanni Dominici, the famous cardinal of Ragusa who was then a simple young Dominican novice, to his mother, "and her words were so profound, so fiery and potent, that they transformed these vessels of arrogance into pure vessels of crystal, as we sing in the hymn of St. Mary Magdalene that our Lord Jesus did to her." A new breath of spiritual life seemed to be given to that decaying city, whose days of political independence were drawing to a close.

As usual, there were those that murmured, and others that professed themselves scandalized by Catherine's mode of life. Some were also appalled at the way in which Catherine was treated, especially in the way that many of the men and women who approached her knelt and kissed her hands.

Two learned men of Pisa came to her and attempted to bewilder her with theological problems, just as had been attempted in Siena. To all their questions she answered simply that only one thing was necessary: to know that Christ, the true Son of God, had assumed human nature for our salvation, and had suffered and died for our liberation. She spoke to them so sweetly of the love of Him that they were moved to tears.

Still, the comments about the reverence shown to Catherine continued to increase, so much so that Fra Raimondo hinted to her that she should prevent it from happening, asking her if perhaps the people's reverence caused her to glory too much in herself. "I hardly notice what they do," she replied to him, "and, through God's grace, it does not please me. I only consider the good affection that brings them to me, and thank the Divine Goodness that moves them to do it, praying that God may perfect and fulfill those desires that He has inspired."

Criticizing the Reformer

Catherine was not the first person to cause scandal while living a holy, albeit unorthodox or nontraditional, life. Most of the scandal caused by Catherine came from the way that men and women traveled, ate, and occasionally perhaps, lived, together. Some scholars believe that the earliest days of St. Francis of Assisi's movement, when St. Clare joined him and the friars at Portiuncula, lasted more than a day or two—perhaps a period of months— before the men and women were separated in their vocations. It may have been contemporary mores, more than religious conviction, that drove St. Clare to a women's convent. That first night, at least, she was a "brother."

Mysterious Stigmata

Her desires also included to "be fastened and nailed to the tree of the most holy cross of Christ, crucified with Him, through love and with deep humility," as she wrote in one of her letters at about this time. These desires were to be mystically fulfilled.

85

It happened in the church of Santa Cristina on the Lung'Arno in Pisa. Although Santa Cristina in its present form is mostly a building of the nineteenth century, prosaic in both its surroundings and its interior, there still stands by the first altar to the right of the entrance a fragment of one of the pillars of the older church, with the inscription: *Signavit Dominus servam suam Catharinam hic signis redemptionis nostrae.* "Here the Lord signed His servant Catherine with the signs of our redemption." It was in this place, on the fourth Sunday of Lent 1375, that Catherine of Siena received the same mystical revelation that had been stamped on Francis of Assisi, while she was rapt in ecstasy after communion.

Fra Raimondo and the others saw her rise up gradually from her prostrate position to her knees, face glowing, stretch out her arms, and then after remaining there for a moment, fall suddenly to the ground as though she had been mortally wounded. She said only a little while later: "I saw the crucified Lord coming down to me in a great light, and for this, my body was constrained to rise. Then, out of the marks of His most sacred wounds, I saw five blood-red rays coming down upon me, directed towards the hands and feet and heart of my body. Perceiving the mystery, I exclaimed: *Oh, Lord my God, I beg you, do not let the marks appear on my body!* While I was still speaking, before the rays reached me, they changed their blood-red color to splendor and in the semblance of pure light they came to the five places of my body. So great is the pain that I endure in these five places, but especially within my heart, that unless the Lord works a new miracle it seems impossible to me that the life of my body may stay with such agony; it will surely end in a few days."

They brought her back to her room in what appeared to be a condition near death. But it seemed that, in answer to the prayers of many, her strength was renewed on the following Sunday after she received the blessed sacrament again from Raimondo's hands. As he tells it in the *Legenda*, he said to her: "Mother, does the pain still last, from the wounds that were made in your body?" And she answered him, "The Lord has heard your prayers, and those wounds not only do not afflict me, but they even fortify it, so that instead of receiving torment from them, I feel them still but they bring me strength."

The Pope and Catherine

It has frequently been stated that Catherine had come to Pisa by the express wish of the pope, to carry out certain negotiations on his behalf, with the object of preventing the republic from joining the league that was being formed against the Holy See. There is no evidence for this in Raimondo's narrative, and it seems chronologically out of place, referring to what in actuality happened several months later. If Catherine had any more definite mission than that of her Divine Spouse for the conversion of souls, it could only have been in connection with the proposed Crusade; she was apparently planning on using Pisa as a headquarters from which to stir up enthusiasm in Italy by both letter and spoken word, for "the holy passage."

The pope was gradually trying to feel his way in this matter. Among the many bulls dispatched from Avignon was one addressed to the provincial of the Dominicans in Tuscany, the minister of the Franciscans, and to Fra Raimondo, empowering them to investigate the will and disposition of the faithful, to enroll those who were ready to give their lives in the great undertaking, and to report to the pope on all of this so that he might know what sort of support he could rely on from Italy. There was some immediate response from individuals, including three of the Buonconti family, but it became imperative to secure the commitment of the heads of the maritime states of the Mediterranean: Naples, Genoa, Pisa, and Sardinia, especially because Venice's commitment seemed doubtful, and Louis of Hungary, in spite of his alleged pledges to the contrary, showed little real disposition toward the effort. Catherine threw herself into this campaign with fiery-hearted enthusiasm and passion.

From the house of the Buonconti, she dispatched letters and messengers in every direction, to princes, queens, and rulers of republics, to captains of mercenaries and to private citizens alike, urging each in his own way to support the papal plan, and to be ready to lay down his life for the cross of Christ when the summons should come. The response to her appeals was prompt. Mariano d'Oristano, who ruled the island of Sardinia, promised to join the Crusade in person, and to supply two galleys, one thousand horsemen, three thousand foot soldiers, and six hundred crossbowmen, for a period of ten years. Queen Giovanna of Naples, for her part, seemed more than ready. "My venerable mother," Catherine had written to the queen, "I will pray to the utmost of my feeble powers for the supreme and eternal goodness of God that he may give you perfect light for this and all your good works. And may you be transported from the sovereignty of this miserable and transient life to that eternal city of Jerusalem, the vision of peace, where the divine clemency will make us all kings and lords and will reward every labor to those who endure it, for his most sweet love." Then she wrote to the queen mother of Hungary, Elizabeth of Poland, telling her that Giovanna's support had been secured, imploring her to use her influence with her son, King Louis, to induce him to accede to the pope's request, and serve the church with his arms.

Meanwhile, the political horizon in central Italy was growing darker and darker. The two papal legates, Cardinal de Noellet at Bologna, and the abbot of Marmoutier at Perugia, were steadily filling the cup of their iniquities to the brim, and the prophecies of Bridget and Petrarch were being fulfilled to the letter.

It was in the summer of 1375 that the Florentines raised fresh objections to the subjugation of their neighboring republics to

Sir John Hawkwood

Sir John Hawkwood (1320–94) was an English mercenary and soldier fighting on various sides and in various conflicts throughout France and Italy in the fourteenth century. He first came to the Continent as a leader of the English armies during the Hundred Years' War; he then stayed, at first, in the service of the pope. But this soon changed and he led his fierce factions wherever he was to find the greatest reward. He was notorious for threatening his own employers with desertion and pillage in order to raise fresh funds for supplies and rewards for his men.

these papal representatives. There had been great scarcity of food during the spring throughout Florence and the *contado*; but, in spite of the express command of the pope to the contrary, Cardinal de Noellet refused to allow grain to be sent there from the places under his dominion. Instead, he attempted to extort sixty thousand florins from the Florentine Republic by threatening them with mercenaries if they didn't agree to the sum. They did not agree, and the mercenaries under John Hawkwood's command arrived at the Florentine frontier.

The pope wrote to the Signoria in Florence, complaining of their unworthy suspicions of him, claiming his great affection for the Florentine people, and urging them to come to some agreement with the cardinal to prevent the soldiers from harming their cities or those of the church. But it was too late. On June 21, the Florentines made terms of their own with Hawkwood, purchasing a five years' peace with him for the sum of 130,000 florins. A few days later, the anti-papal feeling in the city was roused to a height of frenzy by the discovery of a plot (which was apparently revealed by Hawkwood himself) to betray the city of Prato, then part of the province of Florence, to Cardinal de Noellet. Two of the conspirators, a notary and a monk in priest's orders, were tortured to death through the streets of Florence with appalling cruelty. It was also alleged that an agent of the cardinal had been in Florence, spying out a site for the erection of a papal fortress. Hostilities were now inevitable.

Having thus blackmailed the Florentines, Hawkwood came into the *contado* of Pisa and then into Siena, compelling each of them to make similar terms. Pisa paid 30,000 florins, and Siena, 35,500. "In order that the commune should not suffer for what the pastors of the church had wrongly made them pay," the Florentines and Sienese imposed a heavy tax on the priests to raise the money, a levy which, in the case of the clergy of Siena, amounted to two-thirds of the entire sum.

Catherine was apparently still in Pisa while these things were happening. Hawkwood had previously made a promise that he would join the Crusade, and the time seemed ripe for her to call upon him to fulfill his word, and so to leave Tuscany in peace. She sent Fra Raimondo to the English camp with a letter to Hawkwood and his captains exhorting them to abandon the service and pay of the devil, and to become soldiers of Christ. So impressed were Hawkwood and his men that they all took a solemn oath that, if the Crusade really started, they would go, and Raimondo returned to Catherine with their signed and sealed promises to that effect.

CHAPTER EIGHT
Mediating Between Florence and Avignon

To one endowed with the prophetic spirit, it must have been a sinister sign of the times when Catherine saw the cardinals who were created on December 21, 1375. Among the nine new princes of the church were three of the pope's own kinsmen, including Gerard du Puy, the infamous abbot of Marmoutier, who was still oppressing Perugia. Gregory's choice of cardinals utterly destroyed all hopes in a possible reformation of the Sacred College. To Catherine, who had just returned to Siena when the news reached Italy, it seemed like a cruel act of cowardice, like putting ointment on a mortifying wound where something more serious was needed in order to save the life of the patient.

She urges Pope Gregory in a letter from the beginning of 1376, saying, "The sick man is blind, for he doesn't know his own need; and the pastor, who is the physician, is blind, for he considers nothing except his own pleasure and advantage. . . . I have heard that you have made some cardinals. I believe that it would be more to the honor of God, and better for yourself, if you would take care to make virtuous men. If the contrary is done, it will be a great insult to God and the ruin of holy Church." Already the dyer's daughter of Siena could address the sovereign pontiff in terms that were almost dictatorial.

Gregory needed virile counselors. Catherine had hardly returned to Siena when the mercenaries were ousted from Florence. The Signoria of Florence then addressed an impassioned appeal to the Romans. God has had compassion on Italy,

91

he wrote, and has raised up the spirit of her people against the foul tyranny of barbarians. Let the Romans rise, too, he wrote, and help in expelling this abomination from all Italy. Let them not be seduced by the suggestions of the priests that, if they support the state of the church, the pope will bring back the Roman curia to Italy. The example of Pope Urban V has shown how little such promises can be trusted, and indeed, if the pope comes, he will set his seat in Perugia instead of Rome. "Therefore, dearest brothers, consider their deeds and not their words, for they may return to Italy, but only for their lust of domination, not for your advantage. Don't be deceived by honeyed words, and don't allow your Italy to be subject to barbarians or foreigners."

A few days later, Pope Gregory XI wrote to all the states and people of Italy: "We firmly intend to return with the Roman curia to the Supreme City and our other towns in Italy, and to live and die among you, and to relieve you of the heavy burdens that warfare has borne upon you." He then appointed a Roman as cardinal and vicar-general of the church in the papal states, to succeed the cardinal abbot of Marmoutier. But before they arrived, the pope also began a terrible process against the Florentines, which they described as too atrocious even for schismatics and infidels: he enumerated their real or alleged offences against the Holy See, and summoned by name all the citizens who had held office since the insurrection had begun to appear in person in Avignon. A few days later, with Florentine assistance, the city of Ascoli rose up against the church.

Catherine watched this course of events with dismay from Siena. "I am dying of grief and cannot die," she wrote. It seemed to her that devils were carrying off the souls of men on every side. She admitted to the full iniquities and oppression of the

92

papal officials, noting that they were the real cause of war, but she also regarded rebellion against the pope as a mortal sin in and of itself. Her soul was rent in two between Italy and the church, between freedom and religion—which explains why the letters she wrote to the contending parties so often seem to show an exquisite inconsistency.

Despite her entreaties, the Florentines made no show of laying down their arms, and town after town in the papal states, including Assisi at the beginning of March, rose up against the ecclesiastical officials and joined the league. Soon, two papal ambassadors arrived in Florence from Bologna and made three alternative offers on behalf of the pope. All were rejected. After that, Fra Raimondo writes, "They ordained that I should go to the Sovereign Pontiff, in the name of Catherine, in order to mitigate his indignation." The friar was supposed to dispose the pope in favor of two Florentine ambassadors who were already on their way. He started about the fourth week in March, accompanied by Giovanni Tantucci and other members of Catherine's household, with a letter of credentials from Catherine to the pope that we still possess, asking the wavering pontiff to make himself the instrument of pacifying the entire world. She bids him, in the name of Christ crucified, to extirpate the evil pastors and rulers, "full of impurity and cupidity, puffed up with pride." Up until now, she writes, the luxurious lives of the prelates have been shamed by comparison with the virtues of many of the laity. "But it seems that the supreme and eternal Goodness is having done by force what has not been done for love. It seems that he is allowing states and pleasures to be taken from his spouse, as though to show that he wishes holy Church to return to her primitive state of poverty, humility, meekness, caring for spiritual things and not temporal ones." Let the pope take heart and fear nothing; if only he will come to Italy and raise the standard of the cross, all will be well. "I, miserable, wretched woman, can wait no more. I am dying in pain at the sight of God so outraged. Don't postpone the peace because of what has happened, but come. For I tell you: The fierce wolves will lay their heads in your lap like meek lambs, and crave you to pardon them, father. I say no more."

But all immediate prospects of a reconciliation between Italy and the Holy See remained dashed to the ground by revolt and continued violence. In response, Pope Gregory solemnly put Florence under an interdict, revoking all privileges granted by his predecessors, declaring the goods of each Florentine confiscated, their possessions and freedoms now free to anyone who would want to take them. Papal envoys from Avignon were sent in all directions, ordering every sovereign and commonwealth to break off relations with the Florentines and to expel them from their dominions. Many states obeyed. Papal galleys were intercepting Florentine ships and making booty of their merchandise. But while these things were being done at Avignon, Catherine at Siena had a vision in which it seemed to her that the divine bridegroom asked her, with the cross on her shoulders and an olive branch in her hand, to intervene between the church and her opponents.

"On the first of April," she wrote to Raimondo, who was in Avignon, "God revealed His secrets and mysteries in such wisdom that my soul seemed to no longer be in my body. I received such a fullness of delight that no tongue can tell it." In the light of this vision, Catherine offered her services to the Republic of Florence as mediator between it and the pope. She did this a few days before Easter, which fell on April 13. She wrote to the Florentines: "You know well that Christ left us his vicar for the cure of our souls. In nothing else can we have salvation, except in the mystical body of holy Church, whose head is Christ, and we are the limbs. And whoever is disobedient to Christ on earth does not partake the fruit of the blood of the Son of God. There are many who believe that they are offering God a sacrifice by persecuting the Church and her pastors, and who say in their defense, 'They are wicked and do everything evil.' But I tell you that God wills, and has commanded, that even if the pastors and Christ on earth are incarnate demons, we must be subject and obedient to him, not for their sake for what they are, but to be obedient to God because he is Christ's vicar." She concluded: "If through me anything can be done for the honor of God, to unite you with the Church, I am ready to give my life, if it should be needed."

Catherine's offer of mediation was accepted, and so she sent one of her closest spiritual brothers, Neri di Landoccio, to Avignon. He carried a letter imploring the pope to imitate Christ, the Good Shepherd, in his dealings with the rebels, to make peace with them, and devote his powers to the reformation of the church. "I beg you, Reverend Father, to give and grant what Neri, the bearer of this letter, will ask you. I beg you to give him audience and to believe what he will tell you. And because I know that sometimes it

---

Raniero (Neri) di Landoccio dei Pagliaresi

"*Of the three secretaries, Neri was the first to enter Catherine's service. It was he who introduced to her most of the people who later became her disciples. . . . He was of a sensitive, subtle, and despondent temperament—a reader of Dante, himself a poet, a man given to self-torment, and, as his later life showed, with a tendency to melancholia. He must have possessed tact, force, and probably charm, for Catherine more than once sent him on important embassies. . . . In obedience to the dying wish of his spiritual mother—who probably well understood his needs— he became a hermit after her death.*" (Scudder 1, 93)

---

is impossible to write what one would wish, if you prefer to tell me something in secret, tell Neri by word of mouth with confidence that it will return only to my ear."

At the beginning of May, Catherine traveled to Florence. The priors of the guilds came out of the gate of the city to meet her, and asked her to go on their behalf to Avignon, at least to secure a favorable hearing for the ambassadors they were about to send. During the weeks that Catherine stayed in Florence, while the diplomatic arrangements were being made, she put herself in touch with every class in the state, and made spiritual disciples in every direction. Although vigorously continuing the campaign against the papal officials in Italy, the Florentines were prepared to yield to the pope's authority in spiritual matters. "Today," writes one contemporary chronicler, "they have left off singing the Mass in the city and contado of Florence, and no longer celebrate the Body of Christ to us, citizens and contadini. But we see him with our hearts and God knows that we are not Saracens or pagans, but are and shall remain true Christians, the elect of God." Men and women thronged the churches to sing psalms and hymns; processions were made through the streets, bearing relics of the saints; and as many as five thousand flagellants passed along, scourging their bare shoulders. The commandments of the church were kept as they had never been before. "This was so spread abroad," writes another contemporary, "that it seemed truly that they wished to conquer the Pope by humility, and to be obedient to the Church."

Simultaneously, there was a resurgence of activity among the Fraticelli, who held that the condemnation of poverty by Pope John XXII had been "the condemnation of the life of Christ," and that neither he nor his successors were lawful popes. Poverty being the law of Christ, the court at Avignon was seen as the devil's church. The sacraments were invalid, the Fraticelli taught, if administered by an unworthy priest.

The Florentines continued to foment rebellion in the papal states on all fronts. In fact, it must always remain a question whether or not the sending of Catherine to Avignon may have been a mere device on the part of others to gain time. The Florentine archives hold no record of this matter,

**The Fraticelli
and Pope John XXII**

In 1317, then Pope John XXII, at the urging of minister-general Michael of Cesena, brought a number of the Franciscan zealots known as Spirituals and Fraticelli, including Angelo Clareno and Ubertino of Casale, to appear before him in Avignon for a doctrinal trial. They were ordered to submit to authority or be excommunicated and burned at the stake. "Great is poverty, but greater is obedience," Pope John infamously said.

and we can only gather what happened from one of Catherine's letters. According to this, the Florentine Signoria assured her that they were repentant for having gone against the church, and were ready to throw themselves on the pope's mercy. Upon this understanding, Catherine accepted the mission in the latter half of May. "It seems to me," she wrote to Pope Gregory, "that the Divine Goodness is making the great wolves become lambs. I am now coming to you at once, to lay them humbled in your lap. I am certain that you will receive them like a father."

CHAPTER NINE
From the Babylon of the West

Catherine left Florence accompanied by Fra Bartolomeo and a number of other disciples. No details have been preserved about the journey, and it's uncertain what path they took. In any case, we know from one of her own letters that she reached Avignon on June 18, 1376.

The bride of Christ and her companions came as messengers from another world into this Babylon of the West. Avignon had changed little since Petrarch had invoked the fire from heaven to fall upon it. "I know by experience," he wrote, "that there is no piety there, no charity, no faith, no reverence for God or any fear of Him, nothing holy, nothing just, nothing worthy of man." The only change for the better since Petrarch wrote these words was that, instead of a strong pontiff enslaved to vice and luxury, there now sat on the papal throne a weak pope, who, in his sincere and ineffectual way, looked for righteousness.

Two days after her arrival, Pope Gregory XI admitted Catherine to what appears to have been a private audience. Only Fra Raimondo was also present. Gregory knew no Italian and Catherine no Latin. In spite of the correspondence that had

---

The Journey to Avignon

"We do not know with any certainty what route they took. Pius II, in the Bull of St. Catherine's canonization, however, speaks of her having crossed 'the Alps and the Apennines' in the service of the Church; and it is therefore most probable that she performed the journey by land. This is also in accordance with local tradition, which affirms her to have passed through Bologna on her way, where she visited the tomb of St. Dominic in the church of the Friars Preachers, and beholding their cemetery, is said to have exclaimed, 'How sweet it would be to lie there!'"
(Drane, I, 358)

---

passed between them, the pope was prejudiced against her; but he was unable, now that he saw her face-to-face, to withstand the magic of her personality. He gave to her a fine house where, for the three months that she stayed in Avignon, she and her household lodged at the expense of the pope.

But the Florentine ambassadors didn't appear, and rumors—quickly accepted and spread by the papal curia—reached the court that new and oppressive taxes were being imposed upon the clergy at Florence. Catherine was amazed and indignant at both parties, the Florentines as well as the church. "Believe me, Catherine," said the pope, "they have deceived and will deceive you. They will not send the ambassadors, or, if they do, it will only be a mission that will amount to nothing."

Catherine wrote an emphatic letter to the Florentines on June 28, begging them not to turn back, but to approach the pope with true humility of heart, "imploring life like the son that was dead." She complains about the new tax on the clergy, if the rumor is true. "I tell you, dearest fathers, and pray you not to impede the grace of the Holy Spirit. You would be putting me to shame and reproach if I tell the Pope one thing and you do quite another. I beg you not to let it happen again."

"In order that you may see how clearly I desire peace," the pope told Catherine, "I put this matter entirely into your hands. Only, please be careful to keep the honor of the Church." And when the three Florentine ambassadors arrived in Avignon by early July, Catherine asked them to come to her. In the presence of Raimondo, she reminded them of their earlier promises, that the pope had put the peace into her hands, and that they could have good terms if they desired it. The ambassadors brusquely answered that they had no commission to confer with her, nor to make the acts of submission that she was suggesting.

100

All this time, Catherine felt that her mission was a higher one than simply bringing peace between the states of Italy and the church. She was in Avignon as an ambassador of Christ, to ask the pope to return to Rome and reform the church. And she continued, at the same time, to urge for what she regarded as the holy work of the Crusade. Pope Gregory heard her gladly, with Raimondo acting always as interpreter. During one of their first interviews, Catherine spoke her mind concerning the shameful vices of the curia, and the pope, after a feeble attempt to rebuke her, listened in silence, making no comment at the end. On another occasion, Gregory questioned her about his return to Rome. "It is not good," she answered, "that a wretched little woman should be giving advice to the Sovereign Pontiff." To which the pope replied, "I don't ask you for advice, but to tell me the will of God in this matter." Again, Catherine made excuses, until the pope charged her with holy obedience to say if she knew anything of the will of God in this matter. Raimondo tells the rest: "Then she, humbly bowing down her head, said, 'Who knows this better than your Holiness, who vowed to God that you would do this thing?' When he heard this, he was over-whelmed with amazement because, as he said, no human being except himself knew that he had made this vow."

While in Avignon, Catherine entered into some desper-ate struggles with the French cardinals for the soul of the pope. Gregory began to make preparations to return the papacy to Rome, but despite his preparations, he still wavered. In the Sacred College, Cardinal d'Estaing was alone among Pope Gregory's French countrymen to support him in the preparations. The rest were either neutral or emphatically opposed to the move. It seems that Gregory, too, was afraid to openly admit his reticence to Catherine in person, and communications between them were then, for a while, confined to messengers and letters. "Tell him," Catherine said, when Gregory asked for another sign, "that I give him this excellent sign that it is my will that he should go. And the more opposition he encounters, the more he should feel a strength increasing in him." In another letter, she said, "Follow the counsel of those who think of the honor of God, the salvation of souls, and the reformation of holy Church, not that of men who only love their own lives, honors, and pleasures. I beg your Holiness, in the name of Christ crucified, to hurry. Adopt a holy deception; let it seem that you are going to delay for a while, and then do it swiftly and suddenly, for the more quickly it is done, the sooner you will be freed from these troubles."

The actual disruption of the negotiations between Florence and the papacy in Avignon finally came from the pope. According to the Florentines, the terms offered them amounted to the desertion of their allies, the cities of the papal states in revolt, and the payment of an indemnity of three million florins. Even to the papal delegates, Cardinals d'Estaing and Aycelin, this seemed excessive, and they proposed certain modifications, to which Gregory responded that he would rather suffer the martyrdom of St. Bartholomew than consent. He sent his chamberlain to Florence with an abrupt order, and his report was formally delivered before the Signoria and a council of chief citizens, raising their indignation and alarm. One day later, the Florentines wrote to Bernabo Visconti to tell him that the pope was now almost certainly coming to Italy, and that it was more necessary than ever to strengthen their forces. They similarly wrote to the king of Hungary, the doge of Venice, and the doge of Genoa, enclosing copies of the terms that the pope had offered. It was decided to confiscate and sell the goods of the churches to raise money for the war.

Catherine would have preferred to leave Avignon sooner, but stayed at the request of the pope, who felt that his spiritual powers were too weak. He wished to have her nearby until the very day that he would depart for Italy.

The French cardinals made one last effort to draw him back from his plans. They produced a letter, apparently anonymous, but which they ascribed to a person with a reputation for great sanctity and prophecy, possibly the Franciscan Peter of Aragon, for whom they knew the pope had great esteem. This letter commended the pope's intention of returning to Rome, but warned him that an attempt would be problematic under the present circumstances, begging him to at least wait until he had begun the Crusade. This letter was shown to Catherine, probably by Fra Raimondo, at the pope's request. She instantly wrote to Gregory to denounce it as the work of an incarnate demon, "the sower of the most deadly poison in holy Church," calling it a manifest forgery on the part of counselors who wish to impede the reformation of the church. "I conclude that the letter sent to you does not issue from the servant of God who has been named to your Holiness, nor that it was written from far away, but that it comes from near at hand, from the servants of the devil who have little fear of God."

At last, Pope Gregory's resolution was fixed. Twenty-two ships, which had been waiting in Marseilles for weeks, were secretly made ready, and Gregory suddenly, to the incredulous dismay of the Sacred College, announced his intention to depart immediately.

On September 13, 1376, Gregory came out of the papal palace of Avignon to return to the seat of the apostles. A mournful crowd watched his departure in silence. At the door of the palace, his aged father, Count Guillaume de Beaufort, threw himself at his feet, saying, "My son, where are you going? Will I never see you again?"

"It is written," Gregory answered, "'You will walk upon wild beast and adder' (Ps. 91:13)," as he passed over the prostrate body of his father. He had learned Catherine's lessons well. Six cardinals remained in Avignon, while the rest accompanied the pontiff in a state procession that moved by slow stages to Marseilles, which they reached one week later. They embarked from Marseilles on October 2, and after moving slowly from port to port along the Riviera, sometimes in rough seas, reached Genoa on October 18. The pope's nerves were rattled by the journey, and the news he received on landing. On October 12, the Florentines had written to the Romans professing astonishment that the pope was actually coming. "And, if he comes, it will not be in peaceful guise, but with martial fury. We are absolutely convinced that his presence will bring you nothing but war and devastation."

The French cardinals continued to exaggerate every report, and urged the pope to reconsider the situation. A consistory was held at which it was proposed that they should return to Avignon, and Gregory was about to give way.

But Gregory's mind turned to Catherine. Catherine and her company were waiting in Genoa for his arrival. She had left Avignon on the day of his departure, and traveled by land, a journey paid for by the pope himself. On the evening of the consistory, Gregory went in disguise to the house of Orietta Scotti, where Catherine was staying. She fell at his feet, and he promptly asked her to rise, for he was the suppliant. After a long conversation with her, Gregory departed full of edification and courage to proceed. He informed the cardinals at once, and ordered the fleet to be put back to sea. He set sail from Genoa on October 29, setting a southerly course. After several stops along the way, the pope reached the papal states on December 5, landing at the port of Corneto.

At Corneto, Gregory stayed for nearly six weeks in order to celebrate Christmas, as well as to come to terms with the Romans, whom the Florentines were still inciting to insurrection. During this time, he received a letter from Catherine, who had returned to Siena. On December 21, an agreement was made between Cardinals d'Estaing, Corsini, and Tebaldeschi, in the name of the church, and the government and people of Rome. In the agreement, the full dominion of the city was offered to the cardinals, who represented the pope, and the pope agreed to maintain the Signoria of the Bandaresi. All obstacles to the return of the sovereign pontiff to the seat of the apostles had been removed. On January 16, 1377, they sailed up the Tiber to San Paolo fuori le Mura, where they were received with enthusiasm and exultation by the Bandaresi and people of Rome. The next day, Gregory made his triumphal entry into the Eternal City.

It is evident from Catherine's letters that she had no interest in seeing Pope Gregory's return to Rome as a *temporal sovereign*. She dreamed of the pope as a purely spiritual power, coming unarmed in poverty and humility, conquering the opposition by the might of love alone. The spectacle of the church fighting against the Italians with the aid of mercenaries was an utter horror to her, a veritable war against God.

Shortly after his return to Rome, Catherine addressed a letter to Pope Gregory. She expressed the vision that Catholics have often had for their church, praying that their pastors might realize that Christ's kingdom is not of this world, and that temporal power is not Christ's way. These expressions, however, have usually been met by papal declarations saying that he who sits on the throne of the fisherman cannot renounce what the church has come to possess, or claimed to possess, as her own. To Gregory, Catherine wrote: "It seems to me that one must still guard what is most dear. The treasure of the church is the blood of Christ, and this blood is not paid for temporal substance, but for the salvation of the human race. It is better to let go of the mire of temporal things than to lose the gold of spiritual things."

Almost all the states of Italy, even those at war with the Holy See, sent ambassadors to congratulate the pope on his arrival. The Sienese were among those who had to make excuses for their having joined the league of rebellion, and more importantly, three Florentine ambassadors arrived in Rome on January 26. They were the same three who had been to Avignon, and they came with a message to congratulate the pope and to ask for peace.

The pope received the ambassadors kindly, but only offered them the same terms as before: they must pay an indemnity of more than a million florins to the apostolic treasury within four years, and virtually abandon their colleagues in the league. The excessiveness of Gregory's demands was combined with an appalling event that happened a few days later, making any chances of a quick resolution unlikely.

War had continued in Bologna, north of Rome, and then the cardinal of Geneva had taken the papal soldiers to winter in the town of Cesena. The brutality of these ruffians led to an armed uprising in Cesena on February 1, in which three or four hundred of the papal troops were killed. Hawkwood and his mercenaries were hurrying to join the effort on the side of the church, despite a growing feeling among those in the uprising that rebellion against the papacy was no longer urgent. To some, the matter seemed somewhat settled. But on February 3, a massacre began in Cesena. Men, women, and children were slaughtered indiscriminately. The English, led by Hawkwood, were mostly bent on plunder, but others led by the cardinal of Geneva were thirsting for vengeance, and they committed horrors beyond description. The churches were also desecrated, while friars who attempted to give sanctuary to fugitives were murdered with the rest. At least four thousand died, and a thrill of horror ran through all Italy, as horrors were quickly assigned to mercenary soldiers acting on behalf of the church.

"Nero himself never committed such cruelty," writes one Franciscan chronicler in Bologna. "It was enough to make people no longer believe in popes or cardinals."

The Florentines again hardened their resolve never to trust the pope. "This is the unhappy fate of people who obey the Church!" one of them wrote to the other states in Italy.

Nowhere in Catherine's letters does she make any explicit reference to the massacre at Cesena. But the fresh remembrance of these victims at the hands of the pastors of the church must have given urgency to her letter to Pope Gregory that was written ten weeks after the event: "Have mercy on so many souls and bodies that are perishing. O pastor and keeper of the cellar of the blood of the Lamb, don't allow trouble or shame or the abuse that you might be receiving draw you away, nor the perverse counselors of the devil who counsel you toward wars and miseries. Consider what great evils are resulting from this wicked war, and how great is the good that will be the result of peace."

CHAPTER TEN

The Angel of Peace

Soon after these events, Catherine returned to Siena—on April 25, 1377, the feast of St. Mark. She took up her apostolic mission again, working for the conversion of souls, making peace between enemies, tending and comforting the afflicted. Above all, at this time, she was drawn to prisoners. Since the government lived in daily apprehension of conspiracies, the prisons were full, and executions almost constant.

The most famous of these incidents—immortalized by Il Sodomo (Giovanni Antonio Bazzi)'s fresco as well as Swinburne's poem—was that of a young Perugian noble, Niccolo di Toldo. Niccolo was attached to the household of the senator of Podesta and was sentenced to death for some rash words he had said against the state. Fra Tommaso Caffarini found him in the prison of the commune, raging with despair, refusing to make his confession or to hear a word about the salvation of his soul. He had never received the sacraments since his first communion.

Then Catherine went to see him in his cell. As Fra Tommaso explains, he became "like a meek lamb led to the sacrifice," and went to his execution with Christ's name and Catherine's name on his lips. Catherine actually received Niccolo's severed head in her very hands when it was over.

In one of her most beautiful and famous letters, Catherine writes to Fra Raimondo describing the final end of this young noble, unjustly doomed to die by the government of Siena:

I went to visit him, and he confessed, and he disposed himself very well. He made me promise by the love of God that, when the time of execution came, I would be with him. And so I promised that I would. Then in the morning, before the bell tolled, I went to him again and he received great consolation. I brought him to hear Mass and he received Holy Communion. That will of his was harmonized with and subjected to the will of God, and there only remained a fear of not being strong at the last moment. . . . He said to me, "Stay with me, and do not abandon me, and I shall die contently." And he leaned his head on my breast. . . . When I began to feel his fear, I said, "Take heart, sweet brother of mine, for soon you will come to the marriage feast. You will be bathed in the sweet blood of the Son of God, with the sweet name of Jesus, and I will be waiting for you at the place of execution." . . . I awaited him, then, at the place of execution, and I stayed there with continual prayer. Before he arrived, I placed myself down and stretched out my neck on the block; but nothing was done to me, for I was full of love of myself. Then I prayed and said to Mary that I wished for this grace, that she would give him true light and peace of heart at that moment. . . . Then he came and placed himself down with great meekness, and I stretched out his neck, and bent down over him, and reminded him of the blood of the Lamb. His mouth said nothing but "Jesus" and "Catherine," and as he spoke these words, I received his head into my hands, closing my eyes in the Divine Goodness and saying: "I will."

Swinburne's Poem
Algernon Charles Swinburne's (1837–1909) poem "Siena" is a lyrical tribute to the city itself, and contains many verses about Catherine, including these about her care for Niccolo, her work to

"He met his death," writes Fra Tommaso, "with such wonderful devotion that it seemed not that of a condemned man, but rather, the passing away of some holy martyr. All who witnessed it, among whom I was one, were moved to such intense compunction of heart that never, until then, do I remember having been present at any funeral where there was so much devotion."

Eating souls, or devouring demons, were Catherine's playful terms for converting sinners. "We must work for the honor of God, just as the holy apostles once did," she writes to two of her women friends. Elsewhere, she wrote to her mother, Lapa: "You know, dearest mother, that I have been placed on earth for nothing else but the honor of God and the salvation of souls. To this the Creator has called me."

Still, she heard murmuring criticism from many quarters. While she spent time in Montepulciano, some declared that she and Raimondo were plotting with the Salimbeni against the state, and so Tommaso di Guelfaccio arrived with a letter ordering them to return to Siena. In her answer, a long and eloquent letter, Catherine rebuked their self-love and cowardly fear that was

return the papacy from Avignon, and her fiery letter writing:

And the house midway hanging see
That saw Saint Catherine bodily,
Felt on its floors her sweet feet move,
And the live light of fiery love
Burn from her beautiful strange face,
As in the sanguine sacred place
Where in pure hands she took the head
Severed, and with pure lips still red
Kissed the lips dead.

For year through, sweetest of
    the saints,
In quiet without cease she wrought,
Till cries of men and fierce complaints
From outward moved her maiden
    thought;
And prayers she heard and sighs
    toward France,
"God, send us back deliverance,
Send back thy servant, lest we die!"
With an exceeding bitter cry
They smote the sky.

Then in her sacred saving hands
She took the sorrows of the lands,
With maiden palms she lifted up
The sick time's blood-embittered cup,
And in her virgin garment furled
The faint limbs of a wounded world.
Clothed with calm love and
    clear desire,
She went forth in her soul's attire,
A missive fire.
("Siena," stanzas 5–7)

leading them to mistrust those who were laboring indefatigably
for their welfare and peace. In another letter to Salvi di Pietro, a
goldsmith in Siena, she wrote that, in spite of the murmurs, God
had asked her to stay until her work was accomplished, and that
she rejoiced in being persecuted. "Whether the demon likes it
or not, I will continue to exercise my life to the honor of God
and the salvation of souls, for the entire world and particularly
for my native city. But Siena does a shameful thing in believing
or imagining that we are engaged in weaving plots in the lands
of the Salimbeni, or in any other place in the world."

It was at this time that Catherine was asked, to her great
sorrow, to let Raimondo go to serve the pope. She sent him "with
certain proposals," he recounts, "that would have been good for
the holy Church of God, if they had been understood," and at
Rome, the general of their order compelled him to resume the
office of prior of the Minerva, a position he had held under
Pope Urban V. He was unable to return to Catherine. Except for
a few weeks, she was never again to be reunited with her "most
beloved and most dear father and son in Jesus Christ, given to
me by that sweet Mother Mary." His spiritual aid had been a
consolation to her for three years; she had been able to confide
in him as she was able to confide in no one else; and the parting
was a great loss to her.

Sometime around the beginning of the new year, 1378,
Catherine seems to have returned to Siena. But again, her stay
was brief. Almost as soon as she arrived, she received an order
from the pope, through Fra Raimondo, to go to Florence. Even
though negotiations had ruptured the previous October, neither
party had entirely abandoned hope of a compromise. The
financial position of both the Florentines and the church was
desperate. Before Raimondo had left Tuscany, Niccolo Soderini

had come to Siena and assured him that the majority of the Florentines sincerely desired peace, but were prevented from it by the actions of a minority in the government.

At about this time, Pope Gregory explained his desperation in a brief to his papal nuncio in Naples. No tongue or pen, he writes, can adequately express his urgent needs; the provinces are in anarchy, the mercenaries are clamoring for pay, he is tormented inside, and even Queen Giovanna herself seems to begin to favor the enemies of the church.

Gregory's counsels had been further weakened by the loss of his loyal and strenuous Cardinal d'Estaing, who died the previous November. In early 1378, Gregory had even taken the extreme step of appealing to Bernabo Visconti, and sent the bishop of Urbino to propose him to the Florentines as an arbitrator. And he continued to put his hope in Catherine.

"It has been written to me," Pope Gregory said to Fra Raimondo, "that if Catherine of Siena goes to Florence, I will have peace." Raimondo answered that they were all ready, in obedience to his Holiness, to face martyrdom. "I do not wish you to go," replied the pope, "because they would maltreat you; but I do not believe that they would harm Catherine, for she is a woman and they hold her in reverence."

At the pope's request, Raimondo at once drew up the necessary bulls and credentials and dispatched them to Catherine, who, "like a daughter of true obedience," instantly left for Florence.

The exact date is uncertain, but it was no later than the beginning of March 1378 that Catherine found herself within the walls of Florence for the third time. It is clear that her mission on behalf of the pope was less to the people as a whole, than it was to the Parte Guelfa, whom Gregory hoped to win

Who Were the Parte Guelfa?

The Italian phrase "Parte Guelfa" literally means the leaders or government party ruling Florence. It is a term that refers to the office of the government, rather than one leader in particular. In Catherine's day, the Parte Guelfa saw the rise of a new oligarchy and the fall of the old guilds as the centers of power in Florence. In Florence today, one can visit the Palagio di Parte Guelfa, located in the Piazza di Parte Guelfa; palagio simply means "palace," as in the "Palace of the Florentine government." This was the most honored and protected place in all of Renaissance-era Florence. Just a few years after these incidents involving St. Catherine, "in 1386, the Parte Guelfa, stronghold of the elite enemies of the popolo, had built a new palace that faced the piazza from its northwest corner near the beginning of via de'Calzaiuoli . . . a celebration of the power and prestige of the elite that had regained the reins of government in the 1380s and 1390s" (Crum, 37).

over. Following the hint that Niccolo Soderini had given to Fra Raimondo, she was to use her moral influence to prevent the extreme spirits on the opposite side from interrupting the peace negotiations that had already begun. To avoid attracting notice and exciting anticlerical feelings, none of Catherine's usual friars and priests, except for Fra Santi, came with her. Besides Lisa and Giovanna di Capo, her only other companions appear to have been Neri and Stefano.

This is one of the few episodes in Catherine's life for which we have external, contemporary (and for once, hostile) evidence. "It happened that there was in Florence a woman named Catherine," begins Marchionne Stefani's account, "the daughter of Giacomo Benincasa, who was holy, pure, and chaste, began to blame the opponents of the Church. Those who managed the Party welcomed her gladly, and Niccolo Soderini made a room for her in his house; he and many others praised her to the skies."

Marchionne continues: "It is true that she knew ecclesiastical matters, both by her natural talents and by what she had acquired; and she spoke and wrote very well. Piero Canigiani, too, was collecting money from all his people, men and women, for her cause. Either maliciously by her own will, or instigated by these men, she was brought many times to the meetings of the Party to declare that it was right to admonish them to stop the war. She was reputed to be a prophetess by those in the Party, and by others, she was considered a hypocrite and a bad woman. Many things were said about her, some about treachery, and others believed that they were speaking well by speaking evil of her."

As Marchionne recounts (and let it be noted that after Catherine's death, he, too, acknowledged her sanctity), as soon as Catherine arrived, she began to urge the citizens of Florence on the need of making peace with the pope. Niccolo Soderini brought her to speak with the officials of the Parte Guelfa, to whom she declared it was absolutely right to deprive of their office those who were attempting to prolong the war. Such men were not rulers, she said, but destroyers of the city. As a result, the captains of the party readily agreed to put all possible pressure upon the Signoria to work for peace, "not only with words, but with deeds."

Among the Florentines who became Catherine's disciples at this time were two of special note: Barduccio di Piero Canigiani and Giannozzo di Benci Sacchetti. Barduccio was a consumptive youth who began to cling to Catherine with both heart and soul. He entered her spiritual family as one of her secretaries and never again left her. "He was young in years but old in life," writes Fra Raimondo. "The sacred virgin loved him, it seemed to me, more tenderly than the others, and this, I think, was because of his purity of disposition." Giannozzo, meanwhile, was a squanderer of opportunities and a poet of note in the vernacular Italian, whose *laude* were being sung by the people in processions when they were deprived of the Mass by papal interdicts. One of these

The Music of the Troubadours

Laude (plural) were the songs of poets during the late Middle Ages in both eastern and western Europe. Inherited from the troubadour poets, these poems and songs were written and sung in the vernacular by one person, one voice, usually while strolling or processing through a town. St. Francis of Assisi was influenced by them, as were his followers, and the Dominicans, such as Giannozzo, of that time. They converted the laude *tradition to holy uses. Even flagellants were known to sing* laude *as they walked the streets of what are now Italy, France, Germany, and even as far away as Poland and Sweden. By the second half of the fifteenth century,* laude *became known as "sacred vernacular music," and all other forms of vernacular music were forbidden in Florence.*

compositions, O *divina carita,* reads like a rendering into verse of one of Catherine's own letters, and another, which begins *Maria dolce che fai,* is frequently attributed to others and is a classic of its kind. Giannozzo's conversion was sincere, but his judgment not very sound. Unfortunately, he continued to fish in the troubled waters of political intrigue, sometimes assailing his opponents with poetical political lampoons, and his final fate was one of the many tragedies that saddened Catherine's life.

Meanwhile, Sarzana (today, about an hour from Florence) was chosen as the place for a peace conference, under the presidency of Bernabo Visconti. The pope was represented by Jean de la Grange, the Benedictine cardinal of Amiens, and two other French prelates of the curia. Venice, France, Naples, and of course, Florence all sent ambassadors. The delegates had already agreed on the amount of the indemnity (less than half of what the pope had originally demanded), and were also close to coming to terms on the other conditions.

The Florentine delegation arrived on March 22, but only five days later, two hours after sunset, there came a knocking at the Porta San Frediano, and a cry: "Open quickly to the messenger of peace!" The guards drew back the bolts but saw no one. Then the cry spread throughout the city: "The olive has come, the peace is made!" People rushed from their houses repeating it, carrying torches, and began to illuminate the city. The priors of Sarzana, not yet knowing any official news to give reason for the outbreak of enthusiasm, ordered everyone to go quietly home until morning. It was a few days later that the news reached Florence that Pope Gregory had died at that very hour. People said that it was the angel of God that had come knocking at Porta San Frediano, but perhaps it was the pontiff's unquiet ghost, seeking a reconciliation with the city that he had cast out of the bosom of the church?

For the first time in seventy-four years, a new pope was elected in the Vatican, on April 8. Couriers rode into Florence with the news that the Roman cardinal, Francesco Tebaldeschi, had been raised to the papacy. Quickly following this came an official notification that not Tebaldeschi, but "the Lord Bartolomeo of Bari" had been made pope, and had taken the title of Urban VI. What this meant and what happened, will have to be explained.

On the news of Gregory's death, the papal representatives left Sarzara, the peace negotiations having thus come to an end without result. In May, the Florentines sent eight ambassadors, two from each quarter of the city, to honor the new Pope Urban, and to conclude peace with the Holy See. For her part, St. Catherine was hopeful of the new situation and wrote in a

The Beginning of the Great Schism

As we will see in much greater detail in the next chapter, Bartolomeo Prignano became Pope Urban VI in 1378, against the wishes of the Roman people, who were demanding one of their own, a Roman, to fill Gregory's vacancy. The College of Cardinals had wanted to elect a man who they believed could satisfy both the Roman people's desire to have an Italian, and the desires of the still powerful French cardinals.

letter to William Flete, "Now, by the divine grace, the people are beginning to be obedient to their Father."

The Violent Revolt of the Ciompi

But in Florence, the dissensions were growing daily more intense. A split began to occur between the two ruling powers: the Parte Guelfa and the Signoria. As the prospects of peace drew near, the power of some decreased and they waxed more arrogant and vigorous in their admonitions. In the background, scarcely heard or heeded by either faction, were the ominous rumblings of a coming storm; the artisans and unemployed of the lowest classes, the *ciompi* (literally: wool carders), were exchanging fierce and secret oaths, preparing the general uprising that was to overwhelm the whole city a few weeks later.

On Tuesday, June 22, the guilds rose in arms and came with their banners into the piazza, shouting: "Viva il Popolo!" The Signoria empowered the magistrates and colleges to reform the city and abolish the unpopular laws of the Parte Guelfa, but in the meanwhile, the populace had begun to take vengeance on their own account. They attacked the houses of the leaders of the Parte Guelfa. Some of the leaders escaped, disguising themselves as friars. But many houses were looted and engulfed in flames. A bunch of men broke open the prisons and released the prisoners, invaded the monastery of the Angeli where many of the citizens had placed their goods for safety, and sacked it and killed two lay brothers.

Catherine was nearly in danger herself, and we can imagine that, given her desire for martyrdom, she was disappointed in the outcome. Raimondo's account of these events in part 3 of the *Legenda*, is clearly based upon what Christofano told him, slightly colored, perhaps, by an unconscious desire to make it resemble the scene in the Garden of Olives in the fourth Gospel. As Raimondo tells it, a band of armed rioters, probably at the instigation of the more embittered victims of the Parte Guelfa, declared that they would burn her alive or cut her into pieces. She was apparently with Neri, Barduccio, and Cristofano in the little house on the hillside of San Giorgio at the time. Those who kept the house, fearing for their own safety, asked her and her companions to leave. "But she, conscious of her own innocence and suffering gladly for the cause of the holy Church, was not at all moved from her constancy; in fact, she even smiled and encouraged her companions, imitating her divine bridegroom, going to a place where there was a garden, and there, gave herself to prayer." Soon the men broke in, brandishing their weapons and shouting, "Where is Catherine!" She went to meet them, and with a radiant look on her face, fell to her knees before their leader, saying, "I am Catherine. Do to me whatever God will permit. But I tell you, in the name of the Almighty, hurt no one of these who are with me."

Their leader hesitated, and then told her to go away. She protested.

"Why should I go away, when I have found all that I desire? I offer myself a living sacrifice to God. If you are sent to kill me, act boldly. I will not move from this place. But harm no one who is with me."

At this, the whole band went away in confusion. But when her companions joined Catherine again, rejoicing that she had escaped their violence, Catherine wept bitterly, saying that she had thought God was about to grant her the red rose of martyrdom, but now saw that her sins had deprived her of that blessing. "I tell you," she later wrote to Raimondo, "that today I wish to begin anew, in order that my sins may not draw me back from the great bliss of giving my life for Christ."

She continues:

My soul feels more bliss than I can say. For if I were to give my body to be burned, it doesn't seem to me that I could possibly be giving nearly as much as the grace I have received. I tell you this so that you may feel delight with gladness, and so that you and I may begin to count my imperfections, since such great delight was prevented by my sins. How blessed my soul would have been, if I had given my blood for the most sweet Spouse and for love of the blood and for the salvation of souls! I will say no more about this: I leave it and other things to Cristofano to say. I will only add that you should beg Christ on earth [the pope] not to postpone the peace because of what has happened—but to conclude it even more promptly, so that he may then carry out the other deeds he has planned for the honor of God and the reformation of the Church. There has been no change because of these events; the city seems to be pacified for the moment. Tell him to have pity and compassion on these souls who are in great darkness; and tell him to deliver me quickly from prison, for unless peace is made, it seems that I cannot get out.

This was probably written on the day of the tumultuous events, immediately after the Signoria had put down the rising with practically no loss of life, except for those who had been executed by the law. "But, although the tumult had ceased," chronicles Raimondo, "the holy virgin and her fellowship were by no means safe. In fact, such great fear had come upon the inhabitants of the city that, even as in the time of the martyrs, there was no one who would receive Catherine into his house. Her spiritual sons and daughters advised her to return to the city of Siena; but she answered them saying that she couldn't depart from the Florentine territory until peace was announced—for so, she said, she had been commanded by God."

The whole city of Florence was at a standstill. There was no *festa* on the Feast of St. John, and for the rest of the month of June the artisans and merchants didn't open their shops, the citizens dared not to lay down their weapons, and strict guard was kept throughout the city, night and day. The presence of Catherine seemed useless, and only led to fresh scandals. After a few days, she and her disciples left the city and went to what Raimondo

The Beauty of Vallombrosa

Vallombrosa is one of those almost magical places in Italian history. Situated about thirty kilometers southeast of Florence, it is a forested area that was believed to be full of spirits in prehistory. The name literally means "shady valley" and is even mentioned by the Puritan John Milton, in his epic poem, Paradise Lost. In 1095, the Florentine Giovanni Gualberto, who later became known within Catholicism by the Anglicized name of St. John Gualbert, build a Benedictine monastery there. The story of this religious place is similar to that of many another religious foundation in Europe: at times flourishing, and at other times plundered or desolate. Vallombrosa Abbey still remains today, but only a handful of monks reside there, mostly as caretakers, for the tourists who visit. It is nevertheless the motherhouse of the Vallumbrosan Order.

calls "a certain solitary place, outside the city, but not outside its territory, where hermits were known to dwell." This is usually imagined to be Vallombrosa, in the Casentino Valley. It is also usually assumed that Niccolo Soderini accompanied them there.

The new Signoria, which took office on July 1, was judged by the people to be composed of "peaceful and quiet men who love the repose of the city and their fellow citizens." They began their duties quietly, without the ringing of bells or similar pomp. They at once ordered the citizens to lay down their weapons, the *contadini* to leave the city or else face execution, the shops to be opened, the barricades pulled down, and everyone to go about his business. And, as one contemporary chronicler puts it, "They were obeyed in everything and in a very few days it was done. The city passed from good to better, and it remained in repose, without murmuring, for ten days." Under these circumstances, it seemed safe for Catherine and her company to return to Florence.

From Florence, she wrote her first letter to the new pope, Urban VI, whom she had known in Avignon, including the harsher side of his character. She urged him to work for the reformation of the church. "Most holy Father, God has set you as shepherd over his little sheep of all the Christian religion. He has set you as the cellarer to deal out the blood of Christ crucified, whose vicar you are. And he has set you in a time when iniquity abounds in your subjects, in the body of holy Church, and throughout all of Christendom, more than it has done for ages. It is for this reason, all the more that you need to be rooted in perfect charity, with the pearl of justice. O sweetest father, the world cannot endure anymore: the vices, especially in those who are placed in the garden of the Church as sweet flowers, to give the scent of virtue, but we see them so full of wickedness that they are polluting the whole world."

Let him begin the reformation with the Sacred College itself, Catherine says, choosing a band of holy and fearless men for cardinals who will aid him in his difficult task and correct the laity only by their own virtuous example. And let him, she says, quickly receive back the Florentines and their allies into the fold. "Oh, my *babbo* [daddy], I am hesitant to stay here any longer. Do with me afterwards what you will. Grant this grace and this mercy to me, miserable wretched woman, who am knocking at your door. My father, do not deny me the crumbs that I am asking for your children."

Finally, Peace

Pope Urban VI was no longer in Rome. He was at Tivoli, alone with the four Italian cardinals: Corsini, Orsini, Brossano, and Tebaldeschi. He needed to make peace with Florence on whatever terms could be obtained. The new Signoria, no less than the pope, was resolved to make peace without further delay, without haggling over the conditions.

Meanwhile, a strange lull seemed to have fallen on Florence. The lowest levels of society, still expecting to be punished for what they had done in the recent tumults, were holding secret meetings and taking fearful oaths, preparing to rise against the burgher government. Not the slightest rumor of what was preparing had as yet reached the Signoria.

At last, on the afternoon of Sunday, July 18, a messenger rode into Florence through the Porta San Piero Gattolino, bearing an olive branch in his hand, bringing letters from Pope Urban and the ambassadors, announcing that the terms of peace had been arranged. The olive was fastened up at a window of the Palazzo Vecchio and the great bell of the tower pealed out over the city, summoning the citizens to a parliament. "Dearest children," Catherine wrote to Sano di Maco and her other disciples in Siena, "God has heard the cry and voice of his servants, and the wailing that for so long they have raised over their dead children. Now they are risen again: from death they have come to life, and from blindness to light. Dearest children, the lame walk and the deaf hear, the blind eye sees and the dumb speak, crying with the loudest voice: peace, peace, peace. Thanks be to you, Lord, who has reconciled us with our holy father. Now is the Lamb called holy, the sweet Christ on earth, where before he was called heretic. Now, they accept him as father, where before they rejected him."

The whole city was wild with joy. An exultant crowd filled the piazza and the priors came out to the sound of music and salvos, and their notary read aloud the letters announcing the agreement that had been made between the pope and the republic. All Florence was illuminated and the rejoicings were prolonged into the night.

But on the next day, July 19, a rumor reached the Signoria that the whole state was on the brink of a fresh disaster. Several arrests were made and, at nightfall, a man called Bugigatto was examined under torture in the chapel of the palace and confessed that there was a plot for a general uprising of the lowest orders on the following morning. His cries were overheard by an artisan, who was hidden from sight repairing the clock of the palace, and he gave the alarm. On the morning of Tuesday, July 20, the whole populace was up in arms once again and the disastrous revolution of the *ciompi*—the unskilled workers who, having no guild of their own, were deprived of political rights—burst again like a tidal wave over Florence. In the anarchy of those next few days, one portion of the mob sacked and burned the houses of the wealthy citizens who were not their supporters, while another seized on those whom they regarded as their friends and, willingly or unwillingly, made them knights in the name of the people. On the evening of the second day, the Podesta surrendered the palace and the banners of the guilds were hung out from its windows. One day later, the Signoria abandoned the Palazzo

The popolo minuto *were the lowest level of craftsmen and day laborers, forbidden by law to organize into one of the guilds that would have given them many basic rights. Guild membership was also a prerequisite for holding political office, and so the* popolo minuto *were excluded from involvement in deciding the rules and policies that affected them as much as any other Florentine.*

Vecchio and the mob swept in in triumph, while the bells of the tower pealed out in honor of the victory of the *popolo minuto*.

A wool carder, Michele di Lando, who had served the republic as a crossbowman in the wars, carried the banner of justice into the palace. The people declared him the lord of Florence. This man basically saved the state; finding himself its sole ruler, he instantly issued a proclamation that the ravages and brutalities of the insurgents must cease, and summoned a parliament where he was confirmed until the end of August. On August 1, the priors went through the city in the morning, with trumpets and other instruments, which "mightily reassured those who wished to live in peace," according to one chronicler, and a thousand crossbowmen marched through in the afternoon as it was proclaimed that every merchant could return in safety to carry on his business. Heavy penalties were instituted against any who molested another. That evening, the news came that the peace with the pope had been signed and that the absolution would soon arrive.

With the conclusion of peace between Florence and the Holy See, Catherine's second great political work was done. In spite of the great personal danger that she and her followers must have run from the blind hatred of the populace, she had remained in the city all through these tumultuous days of revolution and anarchy. Then she gathered her followers around her and announced her intention of returning instantly to Siena, now that she had fulfilled the command of Christ and his vicar. It was probably on August 2 that she looked her last upon Florence and went quietly home.

There still exists, among the Strozzi manuscripts of the Biblioteca Nazionale of Florence, a fourteenth-century copy of the letter that Catherine addressed on this occasion to the

Gonfaloniere and priors of the republic. It is her farewell to Florence: "You have the desire of reforming your city, but I tell you that this desire will never be fulfilled unless you strive to throw to the ground the hatred and rancor of your hearts and your love of yourselves—that is, unless you think not of yourselves alone but of the universal welfare of all the city."

CHAPTER ELEVEN
The Beginning of Schism in the Church

We must now turn back to what was happening in Rome and Tivoli while Catherine was engaged in the work of God in Florence—and discover how the recent change in the papacy would soon lead to a profound schism in the church. As we have already seen, Pope Gregory XI had returned the papacy to Rome, but broken down in health and embittered in spirit. One of the pope's household told Alfonso da Vadaterra, who was then in Rome promoting the canonization of St. Bridget, that Gregory intended to yield to the pleadings of the French cardinals and to return to Avignon. "I am absolutely certain," answered the hermit-bishop, "that he will never be able to do this; for I know that it is the will of God that our Pope and his Curia remain in Rome." A few days after this conversation, Gregory's last illness came upon him. The Bandaresi forced their way to his bedside to see for themselves if he was really dying. "The Pope cannot survive," one was heard to say to another as they left the palace, "and the time has come for us to be good Romans. Let us now be sure that the papacy remains with our nation."

From his deathbed, Gregory issued a bull empowering the cardinals to proceed immediately to the election of his successor without summoning or awaiting their absent colleagues. They were to ratify the choice that would be made by two-thirds of those present, even in the face of an obstinate and hostile minority. About the same time, he secretly sent after dark for Pierre

Gandelin, the Provencal governor of the Castello Sant'Angelo, and committed to his care a large portion of the papal treasures, forbidding him to give up the keys of the fortress, no matter what happens, without an express order from the Avignon cardinals. This last French pope recognized by the church died on March 27, 1378.

According to one contemporary account, Gregory XI's death was a direct intervention of God to prevent him from returning the papacy to Avignon. According to another, a fearful tempest was about to break upon the church, and Gregory was responsible for it, having lent faith to the visions of Bridget and Catherine by bringing the papacy back to Rome. No sooner was the death of Gregory known than preparations began for the election of his successor. Mysterious meetings were held by the Romans in the convent of Ara Caeli and in the senator's palace on the capitol. Deputations waited upon the cardinals urging them to choose a Roman, or at least an Italian. The same counsels were shouted after them in the streets, and sometimes, threats were added. While the cardinals met each morning in Santa Maria Nuova—which is now called Santa Francesca Romana—to celebrate a solemn requiem at the deceased pontiff's grave, the Bandaresi and other Romans who were present seized the opportunity to tell them the necessity of electing an Italian pope and of maintaining the apostolic chair in Rome.

Then, events escalated. The Romans took possession of the gates of the city, and took action to control the shipping lanes in the Tiber River. While nobles and high officials of the church, who would have relied upon the cardinals for their protection, were expelled, bands of armed *contadini* from the Sabine and Alban hills came into the city and began to threaten the French retainers and servants of the Sacred College. Clearly, the cardinals and other leaders of the church were somewhat trapped.

Nevertheless, the cardinals didn't appear to believe in the seriousness of the danger. They didn't think it necessary to summon their own mercenaries for defense; eight hundred of them were within easy distance of Rome and could have been called. To each persistent supplication to select an Italian, they answered in general terms that they would elect one who would be best for Italy and all of Christendom. The four Italian cardinals actually rebuked the Roman officials for their conduct, but without result. The senator of Rome, Guido de Pruinis, along with the Bandaresi, undertook the protection of the conclave in the name of the republic. A proclamation was made threatening all disturbers of the peace with death—and a block, with the axe and other ghastly implements of the executioner's craft—was solemnly set up in the piazza at St. Peter's. A general sense of alarm and expectancy pervaded the Eternal City.

There were sixteen cardinals then in Rome, of whom ten were French, four were Italians, one an immediate subject of the emperor, and one a Spaniard. They were divided into three parties: the Limousin, the French, and the Italian factions. The Limousin faction was composed of prelates connected by birth or other ties with the families of Clement VI, Innocent VI, and Gregory XI, and who desired to elect one of their own to carry on the bad traditions that had put their own ecclesiastics at the head of the clerical world. To it belonged the cardinal of Limoges, the cardinal of Poitiers, the cardinal of Marmoutier (Gerard du Puy), Cardinal Guillaume d'Aigrefeuille, Cardinal Pierre de Vergne, who were all from the Limousin region of France, and the cardinal of Viviers, who was from Cahors. The cardinals of Viviers and of Poitiers seem to have been the candidates most favored by this group.

Opposed to them was the so-called French faction, which included the cardinal of Glandeves, the cardinal of Sant'Eustachio, the cardinal of Sant'Angelo (Guillaume de Noellet), and the cardinal of Brittany. To this faction also belonged the two strongest personalities of the Sacred College at that time, although neither of them was a Frenchman: Cardinal Robert of Geneva, the "butcher of Cesena"; and the cardinal of Aragon, Pedro de Luna. Robert was the younger son of Count Amedee III of Geneva, and also connected to the royal house of France. The special aim of the French faction was to free the church from the domination of the Limousin faction, even at the cost of electing an Italian pope.

The leader of the four Italian cardinals was also the dean of the cardinal bishops: Piero Corsini, cardinal of Florence. Gregory XI had made him bishop of Porto, from which he is sometimes called the cardinal of Porto. He was a man of great ability and little moral courage. Also in this grouping, Francesco Tebaldeschi was a Roman of humble birth who had been, like the aristocratic Corsini, one of the cardinals of Urban V. Tebaldeschi was spoken of as the "cardinal of St. Peter's" because of his role as archpriest of the basilica. He was an old man, broken down in health and tortured for years by gout. Jacopo Orsini, a member of the great Guelf house, and the only other Roman in the Sacred College. He was dean of the cardinal deacons and a comparatively young man of great ambition. While ostensibly leaning toward the French faction, Orsini was secretly aiming at the tiara for himself, counting on the support of the Roman nobles and people. The fourth member of the Italian faction was the archbishop of Milan, Simone Brossano, a man learned in canon law who had been promoted to the Sacred College by Gregory XI.

In addition to these sixteen cardinals, there were seven members of the Sacred College who were absent from Rome. Six of these, including the brother of Urban V, Anglico de Grimoard, were in Avignon. The seventh, Jean de la Grange, was a wealthy and worldly monk, a subtle politician of influence with the French king. He was in Pisa.

The one member of the Sacred College to whom Catherine turned was Pedro de Luna; he had ultimately supported the late pope in restoring the See to Rome, and in Rome he apparently contemplated passing the rest of his life. A man of blameless life and great charity, there was nevertheless something mysterious and inscrutable in his bearing and character. But of all the foreign cardinals, he was the only one that the Romans loved and respected. He was intimate with Alfonso da Vadaterra, with whom—also with Fra Raimondo—he discussed the situation with apparent frankness. He was reported to have said, "I tell you that, even if I have to die for it, I will choose no one for pope except whom I wish. And why should I deem it an unworthy end, to die at the hands of the people and in this holy city where so many thousand saints have battled for the truth?"

But there was one more person, not a member of the Sacred College, upon whom many eyes were turned in Rome at this crisis in the history of the church. Bartolomeo Prignano was born at Naples shortly before 1320. He had resided at the court in Avignon and was thoroughly conversant with the affairs and administration of the church. As we saw in the last chapter, he had at first opposed Catherine of Siena, and had afterward been impressed by her sanctity. He had come to Rome with Pope Gregory, who had promoted him to the position of archbishop of Bari. In appearance, he was of short stature and thickly set, pallid and sallow in complexion. One of his secretaries assures us that he was "a man humble and devout, keeping his hands free from every gift, a foe and persecutor of simoniacs, a lover of chastity and justice, but one that relied too much on his own prudence, and over-ready to give credence to flatterers." He was brusque and impetuous, easily moved to anger, and lacking in restraint and tact—all traits that had been held in check when he held lower positions of authority.

Bartolomeo Prignano had recently bought himself a house and vineyard in Rome, in order to qualify as a Roman citizen. His detractors see a sinister purpose in all of his movements during these days. He is said to have been constantly and secretly questioning Pope Gregory's physician during the pope's last illness. During the nine days of requiem Masses for Gregory's soul at Santa Maria Nuova, he had taken the opportunity to ask Guido de Pruinis to present him to the Bandaresi and their colleagues.

The Sacred College regarded Bartolomeo as experienced, eloquent, devout, and politically neutral. As a result of his long residence in Avignon, the French looked on him as almost one of themselves. According to the hermit-bishop, Alfonso da Vadaterra, Pedro de Luna told him that he had resolved to give his vote to Bartolomeo because the dissensions between the French and the Limousin factions made it impossible to elect an ultramontane member of the Sacred College. Cardinal Pedro de Luna himself declares that he only intended to adopt this course in the event of the Romans compelling their fellow cardinals to choose a Roman or an Italian. A few days before the conclave, Tommaso Petra told Fra Raimondo that he saw that almost all of the cardinals had agreed to elect the archbishop of Bari, Bartolomeo Prignano.

An Old Catholic Idea:
Ultramontane

As a noun, ultramontane *literally means "one who lives beyond the mountains." In other words, an outsider from Rome. Sometimes, this word has been spelled* ultramontain. *But here, the word is used by Gardner in the way that it was used during the late Middle Ages among those who were jockeying for power in the church in Rome. To be ultramontane was to support the power of the pope in all aspects of governing, not merely spiritual authority, but political as well. An ultramontane pope would be one who asserted his authority and power over kings, princes, and councils. It was only in the late nineteenth century that this faction of opinion finally departed from the Vatican, and the role of the papacy was articulated as only intended to extend over the spiritual governance of the worldwide Catholic Church.*

The cardinals entered the conclave on the late afternoon of April 7, 1378, the Wednesday in Passion Week. Our knowledge of what happened all comes from the sworn testimonies and depositions of contemporaries and eyewitnesses. It is impossible to discover the absolute truth of what brought about the temporary dissolution of the Catholic world.

A clamorous crowd filled the piazza around the Vatican, shouting, "Give us a Roman or at least an Italian Pope!" while the princes of the church made their way into the palace. The conclave was held on the first floor, and a number of the protestors seem to have spilled over, for a time, into their space. The cardinal of Florence, as dean of the cardinal bishops, told the crowd that they would do what should be most pleasing to God and useful for the church. Two of the other cardinals warned them that any interference would invalidate the election. All during the night, a great uproar continued in the piazza and, according to the supporters of the eventually elected pope, it was more like singing and merrymaking, without any sinister intent whatsoever. According to others, it was the clamor of a furious mob.

Early the following morning, April 8, 1378, a band of Romans forced their way into the campanile of St. Peter's and rang the bells. The cardinals had entered the conclave and Corsini was about to address them when the clamor was renewed. The bishop of Marseilles stood and implored them not to elect a foreigner or they would all be in danger. Others present assured the gathering that nothing would happen. Against his will, the cardinal of Florence went to the window with Orsini and one other and addressed the armed and infuriated crowd below, promising that, if they would keep quiet and leave the cardinals to their deliberations, they would have a Roman or an Italian for pope.

It is impossible to say for sure whether or not this promise induced the cardinals to do what they then did. The cardinals of Florence and Limoges suggested that the election should be postponed, but it was feared that this might cause a general massacre of the Sacred College, which could only then lead to anarchy in the church. "I would be willing to lay down my life for the Faith," said Cardinal Lagier, "if God were to grant me such grace, but not for the nationality of a pope." Then Orsini, who was bent at all costs upon keeping out the archbishop of Bari, proposed that a Franciscan should be dressed up in the papal robes and paraded as pope, so that they could escape and hold a free election elsewhere. This plan was indignantly refused by the other cardinals; they said that it would lead the people to commit idolatry. Instead, it was unanimously agreed to satisfy the people, or at least, to take a course that would reconcile the interests of the church with the demands of the Romans.

Pedro de Luna saw the time had come to carry out his plan, and informally suggested that the archbishop of Bari should be elected. The cardinals evidently thought that they were doing their best, although they probably would have made a different choice under different circumstances. They had made a genuine attempt to satisfy the Romans, while not compromising the dignity of the Sacred College. It is questionable whether, at that moment, more than a small minority among them considered the election to be invalid, although the cardinal of Glandeves seems to have protested from the outset that he had only acted from fear of death.

Either to gain time, or because Bartolomeo Prignano, the archbishop of Bari, had not yet accepted his election, the cardinals didn't immediately proclaim the results to the people. In fact, Cardinal Orsini, whose job it was to announce the results of the election, went to the window and shouted to the crowd, "O Romans, if you do not have a pope you like by this evening, you can cut me into pieces!"

A deafening roar of "Roman, Roman! We will have a Roman!" was the answer from the crowd.

The archbishop of Bari, Bartolomeo Prignano himself, appeared on the scene and exhorted the crowd to keep calm, apparently from another window. This done, the cardinals took a hasty meal and returned to the chapel of the conclave to arrange for how best to publish the results. Although he was by now surely aware of what had happened, Bartolomeo does not seem to have been present.

The crowd remained restless, imagining that perhaps they were being tricked. Cardinal Orsini again went to the window and told the people that the pope had been elected: "Go to San Pietro," he said. But the crowd seems to have understood him to say that the cardinal of St. Peter's was now pope, and a rush was made to pillage the palace of Tebaldeschi, an aged Italian cardinal. "No, no!" cried one of the French prelates of the curia, "Bari, Bari!" A roar burst through the crowd, who supposed that Jean de Bar, a hated French associate of Pope Gregory, was the person meant. Brandishing their swords and axes, the Romans burst into the conclave, shouting: "A Roman, a Roman, death to the traitor cardinals!"

Hearing this, and unaware of the misunderstanding that was brewing, the unfortunate cardinals imagined that their election of the archbishop of Bari had failed to satisfy the Romans. Some of them vainly tried to escape, and the others hastily resolved to present Tebaldeschi to the people as pontiff. Despite the old cardinal's protests, they took hold of him and dressed him in papal robes, seating him forcibly in the papal chair, while the bells were rung and the *Te Deum* intoned. His feeble declarations that he was not the pope went unheard, or were taken merely as expressions of humility. They seized him and enthroned him. Prelates and people alike began to kneel to kiss his feet and acclaim him as the vicar of Christ. After a few hours of this confusion and deception, Tebaldeschi was carried in triumph to the papal apartments and left in peace.

As the cardinals fled as best they could from the palace, Bartolomeo Prignano remained in the Vatican, with Cardinal Tebaldeschi and a few Italian prelates. Bartolomeo had had no official notification of his election, but Giovanni Cenci and the Bandaresi had already greeted him as pope, and were busily calming the minds of the Romans. The storm had indeed completely subsided by the following morning, April 9, and Rome was mostly at peace. Tommaso Petra tells us that, at daybreak, Cardinal Pedro de Luna asked him to go at once to Bartolomeo and assure him that he was as truly pope as St. Peter and that he had received a promise from influential people

Te Deum Laudamus
(a Christian hymn
dating to the fourth century)

We praise thee, O God:
  we acknowledge thee to be the Lord.
All the earth doth worship thee:
  the Father everlasting.
To thee all Angels cry aloud:
  the Heavens, and all the
  Powers therein.
To thee Cherubim and Seraphim:
  continually do cry,
Holy, Holy, Holy:
  Lord God of Sabaoth;
Heaven and earth are full
  of the Majesty: of thy glory.

of a place of safety and a sufficient force of armed men to bring him wherever he pleased. To this, Bartolomeo answered that he was not afraid and that there was no need for such an offer, for he wished to see his children freely and had no thought of leaving them. It was then that—either freely or under pressure from Cenci and the Bandaresi—all the cardinals who had remained in the city came to the Vatican. When Cardinal de Luna arrived, Bartolomeo said that he did not want to be deceived, and begged the cardinal to tell him if he had indeed been lawfully elected—to which the cardinal answered affirmatively. The cardinals retired to the chapel and almost immediately summoned Bartolomeo and informed him that they had elected him. "I am not worthy," was the answer, "but I shall not contradict the divine will. I accept." The archbishop of Bari was at once robed in the papal vestments and enthroned on the altar; the *Te Deum* was sung; and the doors were thrown open for clergy and laity to pay homage. From the window of the palace, the cardinals formally proclaimed to the people the election of Bartolomeo, now Pope Urban VI.

On Easter Sunday, April 18, Pope Urban VI was crowned by Cardinal Orsini in front of St. Peter's.

There were some, even in the Sacred College, who were reported to have hinted to Cardinal Orsini that Urban was not the true pope. "Get out of this, you devil," Orsini responded to Francesco Casini when he suggested this, "for whoever says this, lies. He is as much a pope as you are a doctor of medicine." Afterward, the cardinals declared that they were still in fear of the Roman people, surrounded by Urban's spies, and acting under compulsion. Strange stories were even told of ultramontane Carmelites and Augustinians who fared badly at the hands of their Italian brethren for questioning the validity of the election. Nevertheless, it is most likely that the cardinals would have accepted the situation, had it not been for Urban VI's subsequent conduct.

The Cardinals Break with Urban VI

Pope Urban VI entered into his pontificate with a sincere and uncompromising hatred for the corruption of the curia and a zeal for reforming the church. But his vehemence was tactless. Not content with enforcing regulations against simony and curbing the luxury of the cardinals' households, he abused and insulted the individual members of the Sacred College, and announced that he would swamp them by creating many new cardinals among the Italians and Romans. He lambasted them in public, calling one a fool, another a liar, and telling a third to hold his tongue. He once sprang from his chair to attack the cardinal of Limoges, and there would have been a brawl if the cardinal of Geneva hadn't intervened.

The Pisan prior of Gorgona wrote to Catherine at this time: "This Holy Father of ours is a terrible man, and frightens people fearfully with his conduct and words. He seems to have a great trust in God, and for that reason he fears no one in the world and is manifestly striving to abolish the simony and pomp that reigns in the Church of God." But Urban didn't reserve his wrath for evildoers only; the servants of God also took their share of his abuse. For example, we still possess St. Catherine's letter of apology for Fra Bartolomeo di Domenico, one of her earliest followers, who, as she expressed it, "by his fault of manner and his scrupulous conscience" had excited the easy anger of her "sweet Christ on earth."

On April 25, the cardinal of Amiens arrived in Rome, furious with his colleagues for electing an Italian, and openly expressing his doubts as to the validity of the election. A violent scene took place in the papal palace. Urban declared that the cardinal was destroying the peace of the world with his treacherous diplomacy, and the cardinal retorted that if his accuser were still the archbishop of Bari he would tell him that he was a liar. Both the cardinal of Amiens and the cardinal of Geneva then resolved to use against Urban the weapon of the irregular nature of his election. The ultramontane cardinals gradually left Rome, with or without Urban's permission, on the excuse of avoiding the summer heat, and made their way to Anagni (which the late pope had made the summer residence of the curia). They took with them the tiara of Gregory XI and most of the papal jewels. The first to go were the cardinals of Aigrefeuille and Poitiers, on May 6, and the last was Pedro de Luna, who stayed on in Rome until about June 24.

The position of the cardinal of Aragon was a nuanced one. He appeared to be reluctant to break with the new pope, but he too eventually complained about Urban's ingratitude: "The other ultra-montane cardinals have all gone to Anagni," he said to Alfonso da Vadaterra as they walked in his garden, "and why should I linger here with our lord when he will not grant me any of my requests?" And so he decided to follow the others, despite the fact that in his conscience he considered Urban VI the true pope.

Urban seemed to have had no suspicion of the intentions of the cardinals and even talked of joining them at Anagni. He sent the other three Italian cardinals—Corsini, Brossano, and Orsini—to Anagni to assure the French cardinals of his good intentions, "offering them many favors and advantages for themselves and their kin, and to do more for them than any Roman pontiff had ever done." He seemed not to be alarmed when he heard that they were plotting against him, and summoned them to appear within a certain time in his presence at Tivoli, where he went on June 27 with Cardinal Tebaldeschi.

For a while, the cardinals continued to write to Urban as pope and to treat him as such, but this was only a device to gain time. In their public statements, the French cardinals professed themselves astonished that Urban would give credence to sinister reports about their intentions. But in private, they told their Italian colleagues that they regarded the Apostolic See as vacant, and urged them to stay with them. The three, however, returned to Urban.

By mid-July, the cardinals had openly declared that the election of Urban VI was null and void because of the compulsion of the Roman populace, and on July 20 they summoned their Italian colleagues to join them at Anagni within five days. From Tivoli on July 27, a Parisian representative at the papal court wrote back to the rector and heads of the University of Paris that a schism in the church was imminent.

By the beginning of August, Urban had moved from Tivoli back to Rome and taken up temporary residence at the Basilica di Santa Maria Maggiore. Tebaldeschi was the only cardinal in Rome—the other three Italians having gone to Vicovaro at the end of July, and then on to Palestrina, where they said they were negotiating with the Sacred College on Urban's behalf, but in reality they were attempting to keep neutral. Meanwhile, Cardinal Pedro de Luna had undertaken to ask the Dominican friar Gonsalvo to exhort the pope to abdicate the papacy, in order to avoid a schism and in order that they might proceed to a new, free, election. Fra Gonsalvo accepted the commission, but then writes: "I went to our lord the Pope, and after telling him my message concerning his abdication I exhorted him, in the name of God, to dissipate the hosts of the devil that were mustering against him and to take aid from God and the saints. He, like a soldier who hears tidings that the longed-for war has come, rejoiced and answered me with joy, saying, 'In God's own truth, I will not think of laying down the papacy. I will not resign in order to give place to the devil and make sinners exult. No, I will beat them down in the name of the Lord our God.'"

On August 9, thirteen cardinals in Anagni (proceeding without the three Italians) solemnly entered the cathedral. After the Mass of the Holy Spirit was sung, the patriarch of Constantinople preached from the text of I Kings 1:20:

> Yet you are the man, my lord king, to whom all Israel looks,
> to tell them who is to succeed my lord the king.

He declared that the usurpation of the ancient kingdom by Adonijah, the son of Haggith, was being reenacted in the present state of the church. An encyclical letter was then signed by all present and read aloud, denouncing the intrusion into the papacy of the archbishop of Bari, declaring that they had only elected him to escape death. They anathematized him as an antipope, a deceiver, and destroyer of Christians.

Meanwhile, Francesco Tebaldeschi, the last cardinal who had remained faithful to Urban VI, died in Rome on September 6. The Roman pontiff was now alone.

A new conclave was held on September 20 in the palace of the count of Fondi, halfway between Naples and Rome. The three Italian cardinals wished that the election could become a sort of compromise, and proposed to put the decision into the hands of six total cardinals, including the three of them. This was rejected. The cardinal of Limoges proposed the cardinal of Geneva, who was then unanimously elected. The three Italians abstained from the voting, but raised no formal objection. According to Pedro de Luna, they stated that they did this because of the danger that would otherwise have come to them, but de Luna himself believed that they were discontented with the result. On the following day, Robert of Geneva was proclaimed pope as Clement VII. On October 31, he was solemnly crowned in the cathedral of Fondi.

The king of France declared Clement VII the lawful pope on November 16, and Queen Giovanna of Naples ordered the arrest of all of Urban VI's emissaries four days later, paying to Clement the sixty-four thousand florins that she owed the papacy as her tribute to the Holy See. Most of the rest of Italy adhered to Urban, as leaders of the Republic of Florence poured forth the same torrents of fiery rhetoric upon the cardinals and supporters of Clement.

CHAPTER TWELVE
From Siena to Rome

When the first rumors arose of misunderstanding between the Sacred College and Pope Urban VI, Catherine addressed an impassioned letter from Florence to Cardinal Pedro de Luna, hoping "with desire of seeing you as a firm column set in the garden of holy Church, freed from that self-love that weakens every creature."

She wrote: "I have heard that discord is arising over there between Christ on earth and his disciples, and it saddens me greatly. Therefore I beg of you, by that glorious and precious blood that was shed with such great fire of love, never to sever yourself from virtue and from your intelligence. All other things—external war and other tribulations—are less to us than a straw or a shadow in comparison with this."

Catherine returned to Siena on August 9, a few days before the solemn denunciation of Urban's usurpation of the papacy. From her native city, she beheld with unutterable anguish what men were calling the rending of the coat of Christ that was without seam. There can be little doubt that Catherine heard only the version of the extremist Urbanists, and she accepted it unreservedly. "O men—not men—but rather demons," she cries, in describing the cardinals, "how does the inordinate love that you have set on the dunghill of your own bodies, and on the delights and state of the world, blind you to the fact that you have elected the vicar of Christ? He wishes to correct your lives to make you sweet-smelling flowers in the garden of the Church, but you now spread poison, saying that he is not the true pope? This is not the truth, and you cannot prove it."

To the count of Fondi, a few weeks before the election of Clement VII, she wrote that self-love and wicked anger had poisoned and corrupted him: "O dearest father, consider your position and look at your vineyard. In the secret of your heart, you hold that Pope Urban VI is the true Sovereign Pontiff—and whoever says otherwise is a heretic, rejected by God, no faithful Catholic, but a renegade Christian who denies his faith. We are bound to hold that he is the pope, canonically elected, the vicar of Christ on earth, and we are bound to obey him even until death."

These truths that seemed so clear to Catherine, were being rejected by some of those people for whose spiritual welfare she had been especially solicitous. Two of these people—on whom Catherine had placed great hopes as possible champions of Christ and church—were among the first to reject what she found to be manifest: Duke Louis of Anjou and Queen Giovanna of Naples. To the queen, Catherine wrote imploring her to at least remain neutral until the truth is made manifest to her. Pedro de Luna, as well—that pious and charitable cardinal of Aragon—had become one of those who, in Catherine's view, had fallen away. She was seeing the shining lights of even her own Dominican Order passing into the enemy's camp—as when Fra Elias of Toulouse, her zealous and devout master-general, also accepted Clement as pope.

For the next three months, Catherine remained quietly in Siena, dictating to her secretaries her great mystical book, the *Dialogue*, and the letters that she was dispatching in all directions. The dates have been preserved in the manuscripts, showing a large number of letters written or dictated during these months. We find her writing to Pope Urban himself on September 18, urging him to reform the morals of the clergy and to appoint virtuous bishops to surround himself with the servants of God. On that very day in Rome, Urban was actually creating a new college of cardinals to take the place of those who had deserted him, but six of the twenty-nine he had nominated (including the bishop of Autun, who afterward received it from Clement) refused to accept the red hat from his hands. With the exception of Fra Bonaventura Dadoara and the archbishop of Pisa, the others were either men of little note or appointed for political reasons.

On October 5, Catherine wrote to Pope Urban again, when the news of Clement's election had reached her, "with the desire of seeing you robed in the strong garment of most ardent charity, in order that the blows that are hurled at you by the wicked men of the world, lovers of themselves, may not be able to harm you." She added that Urban should fearlessly enter into battle against the Antichrist that the incarnate demons had raised up against him.

At last, Urban summoned Catherine to come to Rome, realizing that the venerated maiden of Siena might be able to help him. Raimondo tells us that at first she pleaded that her constant journeys scandalized many in Siena, including some of her religious sisters. But then an express order came from Urban, and it became clear that she needed to act under holy obedience. She wrote on November 4: "By the great goodness of God, and by the command of the Holy Father, I believe that I am going to Rome about the middle of this month. Pray God to make us fulfill his will." Catherine reached Rome on November 28, 1378, the first Sunday in Advent. Raimondo, who was still prior of the Minerva, met her and her company in Rome, and Lapa seems to have joined them later. On November 30, a Siennesse ambassador in Rome wrote to the Signoria: "Catherine has come here, and our lord the Pope has already seen and heard her. It is not known what he has asked of her, but he was glad to see her. Castle Sant'Angelo is still holding out, and the Romans are bombarding it daily."

Urban received Catherine in a public audience, surrounded by those of his new cardinals who were in Rome. At his bidding, she addressed them, urging them to constancy and faith. "This poor little woman puts us to shame by her courage," he said, when she finished. "What does the vicar of Jesus Christ need to fear, even if the whole world stands against him? Christ the almighty is more powerful than the world, and he will never abandon his Church."

Still, the situation was full of peril. Clement had armed galleys at the mouth of the Tiber River to intercept Urban's communication with the sea, while in the Neapolitan territory and elsewhere troops were being collected to decide the quarrel by force. The Romans had tried to take control of the siege at Castle Sant'Angelo, but couldn't prevail over the vigorous resistance of two French captains. Urban, unable to take up residence in the Vatican, was forced to remain at St. Maria in Trastevere. There, on November 29, the day after Catherine's arrival, Urban issued a bull anathematizing the "nurslings of iniquity and sons of perdition" by which he included Clement, the ex-cardinals, and the mercenaries. He was unwilling to proceed against Pedro de Luna and the three Italian cardinals, Corsini, Brossano, and Jacopo Orsini, calling them "our venerable brother and our beloved sons." It is clear that he didn't yet regard them as his enemies.

Urban and Catherine

There is something heroic in the figure of this coarse-grained, violent, and implacable man, firmly believing in the justice of his own claims to be the vicar of the Prince of Peace. He was battling against the world in what he deemed the cause of righteousness, surrounded by men who were prepared to turn against him when it served their purposes. And Catherine was at his side.

His first impulse was to employ Catherine for the conversion of the queen of Naples, sending her and Catherine of Sweden together as his ambassadors to win her over. Catherine of Siena accepted the mission with alacrity and enthusiasm, but Catherine of Sweden, fearing for her life, absolutely refused. Catherine of Siena scoffed at the other Catherine's fears, saying, "If Agnes and Margaret had thought upon these things, they would never have won the crown of martyrdom. Is not our bridegroom able to protect us? These are vain considerations, which proceed from lack of faith rather than from true prudence." For the present, Catherine had to content herself with sending another flaming letter to Giovanna of Naples, urging the Urbanist cause on her. "I beg you," she wrote, "fulfill the will of God and the desire of my soul, for your salvation. . . . I wrote to you once before about this matter. . . . I would much prefer to tell you the truth in person, for your salvation and for the honor of God, rather than in writing." For a while, Catherine continued to hope that she would be able to travel to Naples and win the wayward soul of the queen.

But another disappointment awaited Catherine. In November, Urban had decided to send a second embassy to France and his choice had fallen on Fra Raimondo as one of the three ambassadors. He set out in early December. After more than a year's separation, they only had passed a few days in each other's company, and Catherine, while urging him to go in the service of the church, felt the separation keenly. Instinctively, she knew that the conversation they had together before he started was to be their last of any real length. "We will never speak like this to each other again," she said. The ship to take him to Pisa was waiting in the Tiber River. Catherine accompanied him to the bank and when the sailors began to row, she knelt awhile in prayer. Then, rising and weeping, she made the sign of the cross as the ship passed away. "She seemed to be saying," wrote Raimondo later, "go in safety, my son, for the sign of the holy cross is protecting you. In this life, you will never see your mother again."

Raimondo's ship reached Pisa safely, and there he received a letter from Catherine written "with desire of seeing you illumined with a true and most perfect light." The friar continued his journey by sea to Genoa, and from there by land to the frontier town of Ventimiglia. Raimondo received a warning that an ambush was set for him and that his death was certain if he went any further. He returned to Genoa and reported what had happened to Urban, who asked him to stay where he was and preach. The pope appears to have been perfectly satisfied with his conduct, but to Catherine it seemed to be a betrayal of the truth, a flight from martyrdom. "God has wished you to know your own imperfection," she wrote, "showing you that you are still a child that needs milk and not a man to live on bread. For if he had seen that you had teeth for it, he would have given it to you."

Meanwhile, Urban had resolved to summon the "servants of God" to his aid, to fill Rome with men of great repute for holiness, so that all the spiritual forces within the church would be on his side. "In this horrible tempest that threatens the Church with shipwreck," he wrote on December 13 to the prior of Gorgona, "We believe and hope to be divinely helped by the prayers and tears of the just, rather than by the arms of soldiers. We summon the assistance of the just children of the church, just like St. Peter who, when he was sinking in the sea sought aid from the Lord and merited deliverance from his loving hand." In this bull, the monk is to have special prayers and sacrifices offered night and day, and to seek out certain representatives of the religious orders. Catherine herself forwarded the bull to the prior of Gorgona. "Now is our time," she wrote, "in which it will be seen who is a lover of the truth. We must rise from slumber and place the blood of Christ before our eyes, so that we may be ready for battle. Our sweet holy father, Pope Urban VI, true Supreme Pontiff, intends to adopt the remedies necessary for the reformation of holy Church—and he wishes to have the servants of God by his side." She wrote simultaneously to members of the religious orders all over Italy, encouraging them to obey the call of the pope and leave their cells to join him in Rome. At the end of one letter, she writes, "pray them most earnestly to do their duty, and not let themselves be deceived by the flatteries of that demon incarnate, the Antipope."

The prior of Gorgona and most of the others seem, sooner or later, to have obeyed the papal summons. Those that came all stayed in the house that had apparently been assigned to Catherine by the pope in the Rione della Colonna (not to be confused with the *Contrada di Piazza Colonna*, where she later took the house in which her chapel is still shown), and lived there as her guests. The number of people who lived in her house was at least twenty-four—sixteen men and eight women, and at times it increased to between thirty and forty. They lived entirely

149

on alms, partly begged in Rome itself and partly collected by her friends and disciples in Siena and elsewhere. Most of them were, in fact, fasting, and ate only one meal a day. Each week, the women took turns doing the housekeeping, so that the others would be free for their devotions. Raimondo tells us that one day Giovanna di Capo, whose turn it was, had forgotten to make bread or to tell Catherine that there was none in the house, but that when the starving servants of God sat down to table, it was miraculously multiplied, so that an abundance was later given to the poor! Catherine herself frequently went through the streets to beg for what they needed, but for the most part, she was absorbed in pressing her spiritual counsels on Urban, dictating letter after letter on his behalf, and in her usual apostolic work among the poor.

Meanwhile, people's minds on both sides were growing more and more embittered. Vague prophecies about the end of the world began to spread about, and there was a strange revival of the doctrines of Joachim of Fiore, who had been forgotten for more than a century. We find Giovanni dale Celle writing to Guido dal Palagio that, although Christ wouldn't reveal the end of the world to his apostles, he had revealed it to the abbot Joachim in order that people might be ready for it, now that it was at hand. Giovanni interprets a prophecy ascribed to Joachim as meaning that after Urban VI will come a Gregory, who is to be the last pope, after whom will come Antichrist, who some say will be pope. "You are young and will probably see all these things," Giovanni tells Guido, "if you live to a normal age."

Nevertheless, the new year of 1379 opened well for the Urbanist cause. England declared emphatically for the Roman claimant. Louis of Hungary and Poland, the chief arbiter of war and peace in eastern Europe, gave Rome hope of armed intervention and assistance. "Through the sweet goodness of God, holy Church and Pope Urban VI have in these days received the most satisfactory news," Catherine wrote in a letter. In Siena itself, the government and people alike had unhesitatingly declared their support for Urban.

CHAPTER THIRTEEN
The Field of Battle

Despite their having taken part in the conclave of Fondi, the three Italian cardinals had not yet definitely committed themselves to either claimant to the papacy. Both Urban and Clement recognized them as members of the Sacred College and sought their allegiance, and they themselves, while appealing to a general council of the church to decide the question, continued to write to both of them as lawful sovereign pontiff.

In the second half of January 1379, they appear to have finally broken off negotiations with Urban, while still abstaining from formally and openly making common cause with Clement. Catherine sent to them, from Rome, one of the most fiery and eloquent of all of her letters. She wrote:

> O how mad you are, to have given the truth to us and preferred to taste the lie for yourselves!

In impassioned words, addressing them as "fools worthy of a thousand deaths," she tells over again the whole story of the two elections, brushing away their supposed excuse that they didn't actually vote for Clement. Had they not consented to Clement's election, they wouldn't have been there in Fondi; for they could have, at least, protested, and didn't do so. "On whatever side I turn, I find in you nothing but lies."

Then, changing her tone, Catherine implores them to return to the fold, and at last, appeals to their national sentiment as Italians.

I have had the greatest sorrow for you three, and wonder at your sin more than those of all of the others. For, if all had departed from their father, you ought to have been those sons who stood by him, manifesting the truth. Even if your father had given you nothing but reproaches, you ought not to play the part of Judas by denying his Holiness in every way. . . . We are in God's hands, either for justice or for mercy. It is better for us to acknowledge our faults and to abide in the hands of mercy than to remain in sin—for our faults will not go unpunished, and especially those that are committed against the Church. But I will pledge myself to bear you in the sight of God, with tears and continual prayers, and to bear the penance together with you, if you will only return to the father.

Nevertheless, the three cardinals—who were together at Tagliacozzo—continued to appeal to a council as the only way of ending the schism, until August, when Jacopo Orsini died. It was rumored in Italy that, on his deathbed, he had professed his conviction that Urban alone was the lawful pope. This, however, was not the case. In his dying confession, signed and dated August 13, 1379, he declares that he acknowledges as pope whomever shall be approved by the church and the council, and expresses his sorrow if, by written word or by work, he has ever done or said anything against him who shall be so declared. It was probably Orsini's hesitation that had prevented the cardinals of Florence and Milan from declaring for Clement.

During this time, both Urban and Clement had appealed to mercenary soldiers to make good their claims to be Christ's vicar. Clement had gathered an army of Bretons and Gascons, and put them under the command of his nephew with orders to march upon Rome. Urban took into his pay a company of

Italian mercenaries that had been raised by the count of Cunio in Romagna. Many battles followed. Meanwhile, Raimondo had remained in Genoa, preaching an Urbanist crusade. But he ultimately failed in his mission on behalf of Urban. In spite of Urban's protests, Pedro de Luna had been honorably received by the king of Aragon at the beginning of the year as legate of Clement, and had secured the imprisonment of Urban's ambassadors.

Raimondo wrote to Catherine, pleading with her not to judge him by her own standard, and imploring her not to love him less because he had failed her again. The saint answers as though she herself had fallen short in love and faith, and been an instrument to spoil God's work by lack of confidence in him. As to any loss of love, she explains that "neither word of creatures, or illusion of the devil, or change of place" can diminish the pure trust that comes from love. Therefore, Raimondo's fears "that the affection and charity I bear you could become diminished in me" come only from Raimondo's own imperfection in love and faith. Still, she doesn't conceal her disappointment that he has found means to cast to Earth the burden she laid upon him: "If you had been faithful, you would not have had all this hesitation, nor yielded to doubts about God and about me; but like a faithful son, ready for obedience, you would have gone and done what was possible. If you hadn't been able to go upright, you would have gone crawling. If you couldn't go as a friar, you would have gone as a pilgrim. If you had no money, you would have gone on alms. This faithful obedience would have wrought more in the sight of God and the hearts of men than all human wisdom would do." She continues:

> I tell you, sweetest father, that whether we are willing or
> not, the present time invites us to die, so that our life may

pass only with crucified desire, and we may voluntarily give our bodies to the beasts to devour. For love of truth, we can cast ourselves into the tongues and hands of men like unto beasts, even as others have done, watering this sweet garden with their tears, sweat, and blood. . . . You commended our Order to me, and I commend it to you, for seeing how things stand, my heart is bursting in my body. Our province in general still shows itself obedient to Pope Urban and to the vicar of the order. . . . It is no time to sleep, but with great solicitude to pray to our sweet Spaniard [St. Dominic] to look down upon his order, which used to work for the exaltation of the faith, but now has become its contaminator.

Others among Catherine's disciples had clearly disappointed her expectations. "Pray and bid others pray to God and Mary, that he may make us do what is his honor," she writes to Fra Raimondo. She mentions one example of a certain Fra Giovanni di Gano, who was apparently thrown into prison. Nothing is known of the matter, but it is likely that he had refused to accept one of Urban's missions to Siena.

Relations had grown strained between Catherine's native city and the Holy See because of the refusal of the Sienese to assist Urban with men and money. We have two letters from Catherine to the Sienese people on this subject, urging them to assist the pope as they had promised, especially now that he was not demanding their aid to recover the temporalities of the church, but simply for the defense of the faith.

There were similar difficulties elsewhere. The Florentines fully acknowledged Urban's election, and turned a deaf ear to the appeals of Louis of Anjou against him, but they were slow in carrying out their part of the treaty, and already behind in paying the indemnity. The Republic of Perugia had concluded a final and complete peace with Urban at the beginning of 1379, but were just as tardy in paying the tribute. It is notable that none of the Italian communes, however dissatisfied with Urban, showed any disposition to desert him for Clement. A few months later, when a quarrel broke out between Urban and the Bolognese, Clement sent a bishop to offer to grant the vicariate of Bologna to the commune on their own terms, if they would recognize him as pope. But the Bolognese answered that, at the bidding of the cardinals, they had acknowledged Urban and they intended to obey whoever should ultimately be decided by the church to be the true successor of Peter.

In Catherine's letter to the Perugians, we find this remarkable passage: "You see these times prepared for great burdens, and our country doomed to the coming of princes—and we are fragile like glass because of our many sins and dissensions. If we desert our father and don't help him, we will be in danger—for, being severed from our strength, we will be too weak."

While Clement was urging Louis of Anjou to invade Italy for the phantasmal kingdom of Adria, Urban was appealing to Louis of Hungary and Charles of Durazzo, his cousin, to serve the Roman Church by depriving Giovanna of the Neapolitan throne. In January 1379, ambassadors from the king had been in Florence, announcing that their master was coming with an army to Italy after Easter, and demanding assistance from the commune. It is heartrending to find Catherine involved in this deplorable business, but it is clear from her letters that she was merely Urban's tool, acting in good faith without the slightest realization of the extent to which he and Charles were prepared to carry out their scheme.

In a long letter to the king of Hungary, who had always been the champion of the faith against infidels, Catherine urged him to quickly make peace with his other enemies so that he can come and defend the church. "Much good will result from your coming," she wrote to him, "and this poor little woman, the Queen, will be delivered from her obstinacy either by fear or by love." Meanwhile, Catherine had sent a last appeal to Giovanna herself, imploring her for her own salvation and for the sake of her people to return to the truth before it is too late. "How can your heart endure without bursting as your subjects are divided because of you?" Catherine implores. And to Charles of Durazzo, Catherine wrote "with desire of seeing you a virile knight, fighting manfully for the glory and praise of the name of God, and for the exaltation and reformation of holy Church." Catherine's letter, together with Urban's summons, was probably delivered to Charles at Padua at the beginning of November, and he at once returned to Hungary to join forces with the king.

The Trial and Execution of Giannozzo

Here we enter into one of the saddest episodes of Catherine's life. In late April, one of Catherine's more prominent disciples (whom we met briefly in chapter 10), Giannozzo Sacchetti, had been arrested, presumably for debt, and cast into prison. On May 8, Catherine wrote to Bartolo Usimbardi and Francesco di Pippino: "I understand that Giannozzo has been taken. I don't know how long he will be in prison, but I am pleased at what you wrote to me, Francesco, that you will never abandon him. And so I command you in the name of Jesus Christ, to visit him often and comfort and help him in all that you can. . . . Comfort him in my name and in that of my family, who all have great compassion for him." Shortly afterward, Giannozzo was set free.

It seems clear that Giannozzo then joined the Florentine rebels in the Paduan district, and by September, he was with the Hungarian army at the siege of Treviso, where he was persuaded to join a conspiracy for the restoration of the Guelf exiles to Florence with the aid of Charles of Durazzo.

Giannozzo returned to Tuscany with letters from the prince, to raise money for the effort. On October 12, he was arrested in a villa at Marignolle and handed over to Cante de'Gabrielli. Examined under torture on the following evening, he confessed the whole plot. His own brother, Franco Sacchetti, was the first to propose that Giannozzo should be put to death as a traitor to his native land. And on October 15, Giannozzo was brought in a cart through the city to the place of execution, and beheaded there. The other conspirators were condemned to a fine of two thousand florins. The king of Hungary and Charles of Durazzo denied all knowledge of the matter, and Charles even declared that the death of such a traitor had been too merciful. It was later admitted that Giannozzo's confession had been made under torture in order to avoid political complications.

CHAPTER FOURTEEN
Catherine's Death

All of this time, Catherine's body was being slowly consumed in her passion for the church. The words of the psalmist seem to be fulfilled in her life: "For I am eaten up with zeal for your house, and insults directed against you fall on me" (Ps. 69:9). Three months in Rome had been for her a time of intense agony, both physical and mental, and of impassioned labor by word and deed, while her infirmities kept increasing.

Toward the close of 1379, Catherine moved with her spiritual family from the Rione della Colonna and hoped to return soon to Siena. "We have taken a house near San Biagio," she wrote on December 4 to Neri di Landoccio, "and we think that we'll return before Easter, by the grace of God." This was the house near the Minerva, in the present Via S. Chiara, where her cell is now venerated as a chapel. It was here that her last mysterious

---

The Head of a Saint

There are many strange traditions related to the saints, especially as seen from our contemporary perspective. The exhumation of their bodies decades after their deaths, for instance (as was done with Padre Pio, Pope John XXIII, and Cardinal John Henry Newman in 2008), often takes Christians of today by surprise. Another bit of strangeness faces the pilgrim today who visits St. Catherine's church of San Domenico in Siena—and sees her head, only the head, on display. One scholar describes the origin of this relic in the following way: "The Republic of Siena sent a deputation to the Pope to express a desire that the body of Catherine should be brought to her native city, so he ordained a 'pious mutilation' and the head of the Saint was severed from the body and being placed in a reliquary was conveyed to Siena. A procession was formed which went forward along the road for a mile to meet those who bore the reliquary, and the whole city in festive attire awaited its arrival. The brothers and sisters of San Domenico who were waiting at the church received the precious relic, which was placed over one of the altars, where it still remains" (Misciattelli, 122).

161

illness came upon her. She endured a prolonged torment of soul and body in this place, offering herself as a willing victim to her divine bridegroom. To those that loved her and stood by her side during these months from January 30, 1380, when her last agony began, until April 29, when she passed away, it seemed to be a new sort of spiritual martyrdom.

She dictated at least two letters to Pope Urban during this time. In one of them, she exhorts Urban to follow the example of St. Gregory the Great and govern the church with prudence, especially in his dealings with the Roman Republic. The Roman ambassadors had just received an insulting message from the tyrannical prefect Francesco di Vico. Catherine dictated her letter through Barduccio:

> I have heard, most holy Father, of the reply that the impious Prefect has communicated for you, full of anger and irreverence, to the Roman ambassadors. Regarding this reply, it seems that they will call a general council. I beg you, most holy Father, to continue as you have begun, and bind them to you with the bond of love. Receive them with all the sweetness that you can, pointing out to them what is necessary, as you see fit. Pardon me—for love makes me say what perhaps doesn't need to be said—but you must know the nature of your Roman children, of how they are led and bound more by gentleness than by any other force or by harsh words. And you know, too, the great necessity that there is for you and holy Church to preserve these people in obedience and reverence—because in that is the beginning of faith.
>
> And I humbly beg you to try with prudence to always promise only what you believe you can fulfill. That way, no harm, shame, or confusion will follow. Pardon me, sweetest

and holiest Father, for saying these words to you. I trust that your humility and kindness is such that you will not despise or scorn the words of a vile woman. A humble man doesn't consider who speaks to him, but looks to the honor of God, to the truth, and to his salvation.

This letter to Pope Urban was Catherine's final political testament. It was written on the evening of Monday, January 30. She had barely finished dictating it when physical pain came upon her, the continuation of a stroke that she had had on the previous evening. Barduccio Canigiani recounts, "After we had written a letter, she had another stroke, so much more terrible that we all mourned for her as if she was dead. She remained for a long space of time in such a state that no sign of life appeared in her. Then, after several hours, she rose up and it didn't seem that she was herself."

A few days later, the rancor that had been steadily increasing between Urban and the Romans came to a head. To Catherine's spiritual eyes, the whole city seemed full of demons. Fra Raimondo pictures her for us, wrestling with the Lord in spirit, begging him that for the sake of his church he would inflict on her all the chastisements that the Roman people had merited for themselves. It is said that the people attacked the Vatican with weapons, and that Urban ordered the gates of the palace to be thrown open, receiving the insurgents while seated upon his papal throne—and by so doing, appeased their fury. We don't know what part Catherine played in this affair, but the reconciliation was attributed to her prayers, and was perhaps due to her direct influence on Giovanni Cenci, the democratic leader of the Roman republicans. In that case, this was her last political work, and surely one of the most noble of her achievements.

Passage from the World

"Then," writes Barduccio Canigiani, "new pains began, and cruel torments increased, in her body every day. But, as we were coming upon Lent, she began to be so zealous in prayer that it was a wondrous thing, with those humble sighs and dolorous laments that drew our hearts from us. I think you know that her prayers were of such intensity that one hour of prayer more consumed that poor little body than two days on the rack would have done to another." He goes on to describe her daily routine during that last Lent: "Every morning we lifted her up after Communion, in such a state that we thought she might be dead, and carried her to her couch. After an hour or two, she would rise up and we went to St. Peter's, which is a long mile from us, and then she set herself to prayer, remaining there until nearly vespers, after which she returned home, so exhausted that she seemed dead. In this way she continued every day, until the third Sunday in Lent."

These are things that are nearly impossible to speak about in the language of modern life. We have Catherine's own words, in the two wonderful letters written to Fra Raimondo on February 15, 1380, the Wednesday after the first Sunday in Lent, the day she took leave of him and of the world. Never was the psychology of saintliness so marvelously revealed by one who had penetrated its depths.

FEBRUARY 15, 1380
The First Letter

In the name of Jesus Christ crucified and sweet
Mary.

Dearest and sweetest father in Christ Jesus. I,
Catherine, servant and slave of the servants of Jesus
Christ, write to you in his precious blood with desire of
seeing you as a column newly formed in the garden of
holy Church, like a faithful bridegroom of the truth—
and then I will think of my soul as blessed. I don't want
you to look back because of any persecution, but glory in
adversity. It is by enduring that we manifest our love and
constancy, and render glory to God's name.

Now is the time, dear father, to lose yourself completely and to think nothing about yourself—just as
those glorious laborers did, with love and desire, offering their bodies and watering this garden with blood,
continual prayers, and by enduring even unto death. Do
not be timid, but be a virile warrior. Don't depart from
the yoke of obedience that the Sovereign Pontiff has laid
upon you. . . . Consider how great the need is, for us to
help holy Church; for we see her completely left alone.
. . . Just as the Spouse is left alone, so is her bridegroom
left alone. . . .

I will tell you what I would have you do. . . . Father
and sweetest son . . . let me turn to how things were
on Sexagesima Sunday [the second Sunday before Ash
Wednesday]. On that day there were great mysteries that
you shall hear from the other letter I am writing to you,
today. But on that day, so great was the pain in my heart

that my habit was torn, as much of it as I could grasp, as I went around the chapel like a person in agony. Whoever restrained me could just as easily have taken my life. When Monday came, I was constrained to write to Christ on earth and to three cardinals. I had help in this, and we went into the study; and when I had written to Christ on earth I could write no more, because the pains were so great throughout my body. After a while, the terror of the demons began, mad with rage against me, as I had been the cause of taking from them what they had long possessed in holy Church.

So great was the terror and pain that day, that I wished I could fly from the study to the chapel. I raised myself up, and unable to walk, leaned upon my son Barduccio. But at once I was hurled down and it seemed that my soul had been separated from my body—and not like it was when my soul tasted the bliss of eternity. [She refers to her trance, or mystical death, in 1370.] This time it seemed like a different thing: as if I was looking at my body, not knowing what it was. And my soul, seeing the pain of Barduccio who was with me, turned to say to him, "Son, do not fear," but I saw that I couldn't move my tongue or any other part of my body, as if I was separated from life itself. I left the body, as it was, and my understanding kept fixed on the abyss of the Trinity. My memory was full of the recollection of the necessity of holy Church and of all the Christian people. I cried out in God's sight, and sought divine aid with confidence, offering him my desires and the pains that I bore. . . .

Then I sought God for all of you, praying to him to fulfill in you his will and my desires. And I asked him to deliver me from eternal damnation. I remained in this state for so long that the family mourned for me as I were dead. All the terror and demons passed away, and then came the presence of the humble Lamb before my soul, saying: "Fear not, for I will fulfill your desires and those of my other servants. See that I am a good craftsman, and like a potter, who mars and makes again as seems good to him, so I do with my vessels. I can mar them and make them again. Therefore, I take the vessel of your body and make it again in the garden of holy Church." And that sweet truth clasped me and turned me round in ways that I will pass over in words, and my body began to breathe a little, and to show that the soul had returned to her vessel. I was full of wonder, but anguish remained in my heart and it is still there. . . .

They brought me back to the room above, the one that had been filled with demons, and those demons began to give me another battle, the worst that I have ever endured. . . . Two nights and days passed with these tempests. It is true: my mind and desire were uninjured, but my understanding remained fixed on these objects, and my body seemed, as it were, to have died.

Afterwards, on the day of the Purification of Mary [February 2, forty days after the Nativity], I wanted to hear Mass. It was then that the mysteries were renewed before me, and God showed the great need that was, and is, still there; for Rome has been on the point of revolting, and irreverence. But God has laid the ointment on their hearts and I believe that this situation will have a good conclusion. Then God imposed on me this obedience, that, all during Lent I would have the desires of our entire family offered up in his sight for the future of the Church, and that I would hear Mass every morning at dawn. As you know, this is usually impossible for me, but in obedience to God, everything has become possible. . . .

I pray that the divine goodness will soon allow me to see the redemption of his people. When it is the hour of tierce, I rise up from Mass and it is as if a dead woman is going to St. Peter's. . . . There I stay until nearly the hour of vespers, and I never want to leave that place, day or night, until I see the people settled and established with their father. This body goes without any food, even without a drop of water, so that my life hangs upon a thread. I do not know what God will be pleased to do with me, but . . . perhaps he will make me rise again with him. He will put an end to both my miseries and to my crucified desires.

Now I pray and urge you, father and son . . . always be cautious in speaking with others. You will seldom have an actual cell of your own; but I would have you always dwell in the cell of the heart, and always bear it with you. For as you know, when we are locked into that, our enemies cannot hurt us. . . . Also, I pray that you will ripen your heart with holy and true wisdom, and let your life be an example in the eyes of the laity, by never conforming yourself to the customs of the world. And let your generosity towards the poor and voluntary poverty, which you have always had, be renewed and refreshed in you, with perfect humility. . . .

Also, I pray that you will gather together a book of all my writings . . . and do with them what you see to be most to the honor of God. . . .

I pray you further, as much as you are able, to be the pastor and ruler of this family, even as a father, to preserve them in love of charity and perfect unity, so that they will not be left scattered like sheep without a shepherd. . . .

And please pardon me all the disobedience, irreverence, and ingratitude that I have committed towards you, and all the pain and sorrow that I have caused you, and the little thankfulness that I have had for your salvation. I ask your benediction.

Now I beg you to labor more zealously, for never before has the Church been in such need. And Christ on earth and Messer Tommaso [one of the papal secretaries] are sending you materials [papal briefs, letters] you will need in order to do your work. And never depart, without permission, from our lord the Pope, because of persecution or any other thing. Take comfort, take comfort in Christ sweet Jesus, without any bitterness. I say no more to you. Remain in the holy and sweet goodness of God. Sweet Jesus, Jesus Love.

As we mentioned above, another letter accompanied the first one, and Fra Tommaso Caffarini declares that this second one was written in Catherine's own hand. Tradition has titled this second letter, or rather, *revelation*, "To Fra Raimondo, signifying to him certain things and new mysteries that God had wrought in her soul on the Sunday of Sexagesima."

FEBRUARY 15, 1380
The Second Letter

In the name of Jesus Christ crucified and sweet
Mary.

I was panting with sorrow, through the crucified desire
that was newly conceived in the sight of God . . . and the
necessity of holy Church which God manifested in his
breast, and knowing that no one can taste the beauty of
God in the abyss of the Trinity except by the means of
this sweet spouse, because we must all pass through the
gate of Christ crucified; this gate isn't found other than in
the Church. . . .

And God eternal said to me, "All this dignity is given
to man by my goodness. But look with grief and sorrow
and you will see that no one goes to this spouse except for
her external raiment, that is, for her temporal substance.
See how she is destitute of those who would take or seek
what is within this spouse—the fruit of the blood. . . .
For love I would have every person give to her, just as I,
God eternal, give to my servants to administer in various
ways, as they have received. But I am grieved that I find
no one to minister to her. It even seems that everyone has
abandoned her. But I will find the remedy."

I cried out in the sight of God, saying: "What can I
do, O inestimable Fire?"

And he replied, "You can offer up your life anew and
never give yourself rest. This exercise I am giving you,
and all of those who follow you. Take heed and never
slacken, but ever increase your desires; for I will surely
comfort you with affection and love and my grace for

soul and body. . . . Devote, then, your life and heart and affection solely to my spouse, for my sake. Gaze upon me and behold the bridegroom of this spouse, the Sovereign Pontiff, and see his good and holy intentions. I permit that, with the methods he uses without moderation, and with the fear that he gives his subjects, he should sweep out my Church. But another will come who with love will give him company, and fill her again." [Catherine's contemporary disciples understood this sentence to fit within the common medieval prophecy of the ideal pope, the *papa angelico*, who is to reform and renovate the church.]

My tongue is not sufficient to narrate such great mysteries or what my understanding saw and my affection conceived. The day passed full of wonder, and evening came. And feeling my heart so drawn by affection that I could not resist it, I prayed, and felt that disposition come that I had had at the time of death [in 1370]. I knelt down with self-reproach, because I served the spouse of Christ. . . . Rising up, with the impression before the eye of my understanding of what I have said, God placed me before himself in a new way, as though memory, understanding, and will had nothing to do with my body. And with great light did my understanding contemplate this truth, that in this abyss the mysteries of holy Church were being renewed as well as all the graces past and present received in my life. All things passed away from my mind through the fire that had waxed stronger, and I attended only to what could be done to make a sacrifice of myself to God for the Church.

Then the demons cried out against me, looking to impede and stop my free and flaming desire. They struck against the outward body, but the desire was enkindled all the more, and I cried out, "O God eternal, receive the sacrifice of my life in this mystical body of holy Church. I have nothing to give except what you have given me! Take my heart and press it out over the face of this spouse."

Then eternal God, turning his eye of pardon toward me, plucked out my heart and pressed it out. With such force he drew it to himself and, not wishing to shatter the vessel of my body, he then circled it around with his strength, or else my life would have ended right then and there. . . . In truth, I was in so great a mystery, then, that the tongue is no longer sufficient to speak of it.

Now I say, thanks be to the most high, eternal God, who has placed us on the field of battle, like knights, to do combat for his spouse with the shield of most holy faith. The field is left free for us, by the virtue and power which defeated the demon who once possessed the human race, and who was defeated not in virtue of the humanity of Christ, but in virtue of his Godhead. With this he will now be defeated, as well, not by the mere suffering of our bodies, but by the fire of the divine, most ardent and inestimable Love. Thanks be to God. Amen. Sweet Jesus, Jesus Love.

In this mystical agony, Catherine passed the next ten days, between her house and St. Peter's. But on the third Sunday in Lent, as she prayed in the basilica before Giotto's mosaic of the *Navicella*, it seemed to her that the church was placed upon her shoulders, and that it crushed her to death with its weight. Her disciples carried her back, in a dying state, and laid her upon her couch, from which she never rose again except once.

"She lay in this way for eight weeks," writes Barduccio, "without raising her head and full of intolerable torments from head to foot. She often said, 'These are not bodily or natural pains, but it seems that I have given permission to the demons to torment this body at their will.' It seemed to be thus, for Catherine endured the most grievous pains ever heard, and it would seem to be profane to tell you of her patience. This much I tell you: When a new agony came, she raised her eyes with joy to God and said, 'Thanks be to you, eternal bridegroom, who grants gifts and graces to me, a wretched woman and unworthy servant, every day.'"

Giotto's *Navicella*

This masterwork is, sadly, mostly lost. Navicella means *"little ship," and the fresco depicts the scene from the Gospels where Jesus asked St. Peter to walk upon the water, toward him, in the Sea of Tiberias. Giotto originally painted it as a commission of Pope Boniface VIII for the Jubilee year of 1300. It hung in the atrium—that is, outdoors—in the old St. Peter's Basilica (before construction began on the new one in the sixteenth century); it was also moved to Avignon during the schism, and ultimately restored in the seventeenth century, to the point where it no longer represents the original work of Giotto. Catherine surely drew inspiration from this painting, in the spirit of upholding the church of St. Peter, and remembering the words of Christ to Peter from that scene: "Courage! It's me! Don't be afraid! . . . Come." And then, when Peter faltered upon the water, "You have so little faith. Why did you doubt?"* (Mt. 14:27, 29, 31).

Last Will and Testament

Tommaso Petra, one of the papal secretaries, tells us how he went to visit Catherine after hearing of her condition in these last days. He urged her to make her last will and testament by prescribing a rule of life for all her disciples, so that each one might know what he or she should do after her death. "Leave us," he said, "all rich in divine love by this last will and testament, for I am certain that this injunction will be most pleasing to the Lord."

Spiritual Implications of Physical Death

It was commonplace in late medieval lives of saints to attribute mystical meaning to the physical torments of bodily death, as if physical suffering was a sign or mirror of a much larger, more metaphysical, spiritual struggle. This is certainly the case in the contemporary accounts of St. Catherine's death, as retold by Gardner. It is interesting to note, however, that the death of St. Francis of Assisi was most often discussed, by his first biographers, without attaching many mystical meanings to the cause of his own painful death. Suffering itself was a virtue, and a gift from God; but the nature of the suffering was described mostly as a natural part of life. In the standard life of Francis by St. Bonaventure, we read these lines: "Through various sicknesses, prolonged and continuous, he was brought to a point where his flesh was wasting away, and it seemed that the skin barely stuck to his bones. While he was afflicted with these grievous bodily sufferings, he would call his pangs not punishments, but sisters" (Bonaventure, XIV, 2).

At Tommaso's request, Catherine summoned all her spiritual sons and daughters who were then in Rome and gave them "a devout, notable, and fruitful discourse," of which one of those present has left an account in writing. It is a summary of what she had striven to teach them by word and deed all of her life:

In the first place, she talked of how she recognized early in her spiritual life the need to give herself entirely to God and to possess him fully. To do so, it was first necessary to strip her heart and affection of every sensitive love of creatures, because the heart cannot give itself completely to God unless it is free, open, pure, and single. She strove to do this with great effort, desirous to seek God by the way of suffering.

She went on to say that she kept the eye of her understanding steadfast in a light of living faith, holding for certain that whatever happened to her or to others came from God, through the great love that God bears his creatures. She acquired and conceived a love and readiness for holy obedience to the commands of God and those of her superiors, thinking that all their commands proceeded from God, either for her salvation or for the increase of virtue in her soul. And she added: "This I say, in the sight of my sweet Creator: I have never in the least degree sinned against obedience, through God's goodness."

Next, she said that God had made her see that she could never come to perfection, or acquire any true virtue in herself, without the means of humble, faithful, and continuous prayer. She said, "Continuous prayer is the mother that conceives and nourishes all virtues in the soul; and without her they all grow weak and fail." She exhorted us to be zealous in prayer, defining two kinds: vocal and mental. To vocal prayer, she said that we should apply ourselves at fixed hours. And to mental prayer, continuously. She also said that, in order to attain purity of mind, it was necessary to abstain completely from every judgment of our neighbors and from every empty talk about their doings, always considering the will of God in his creatures. She added, with emphasis: "We must never judge the will of a creature. Even if we see a thing to be a manifest sin, we must not pass judgment on it. Rather, in holy and true compassion, we must offer it up to God with devout prayer."

Last, she said that she had set great hope and confidence in the divine providence, and she invited us to do the same. She told us that she had found and tasted its wondrous greatness since childhood. And she added: "You, too, have experienced and seen it so great and bountiful that, if our hearts had been harder than stone, our hardness and coldness would have to be dissolved. Be in love, then, children, with this sweet providence, for it will never fail whoever hopes in it, and especially you."

She exhorted and incited us to these and many other things, and asked that we love one another. . . . She also laid this command on us all: "Do not let your desires slacken, touching the reformation and good state of holy Church. But offer tears with humble and continual prayer in the sight of God for this sweet spouse and for the vicar of Christ, Pope Urban VI."

And then, speaking emphatically, she added: "Hold for certain, sweet children, that as I depart in body I have consumed my life in the Church and for the Church." And to comfort us all, who were then weeping all around her, she added, "You shouldn't be grieved at this, but have joy and gladness in it, considering that I am leaving a place of great suffering and going to rest in the pacific sea, God eternal, to be united to my most sweet bridegroom. I promise you that I will be more perfectly with you, and will be able to help you more there than I have been able to do here, as I will be delivered from darkness and united with the true and eternal light. Still, I commit both life and death to the will of my Creator. . . ."

Her discourse was then ended, and she called each of us by name, asking each to do something specific in her name after her death. Each of us, with humility and reverence, received her obedience. Then she asked the group of us, in humility, to pardon her if she hadn't given us a virtuous example by her teaching or her life. She said: "Every failing has been the result of my lack of knowledge. But I confess in the sight of God that I have always had, and have, a continuous and inflamed desire for your perfection and salvation. And if you, my most beloved children, will follow this, you will be as I said, my crown and glory."

At the end, while we all wept, she blessed us each individually, in her usual way, in Christ.

———

This was originally published by Gigli, apparently from a contemporary manuscript, as an appendix to the *Dialogue*. It is clear from textual evidence that this took place many days before the end, before either Fra Bartolommeo or Stefano Maconi came to Rome.

On the evening of Holy Saturday, March 24, Fra Bartolomeo di Domenico arrived in Rome. He was at that time prior of San Domenico in Siena, and had been sent by his provincial on business of the order. Not knowing of Catherine's illness, he at once went to the house and was astonished at her state. Only by bending his ear down to her mouth, and then with difficulty, was he able to hear her whisper that it was well with her by the grace of our sweet savior. The next morning, Easter Day, he celebrated Mass in her room; it was that occasion when, to the

Who Was Gigli?
As Gardner himself explains in the original preface to his biography of St. Catherine: "In 1384, four years after the Saint's death, Fra Raimondo delle Vigne of Capua, who had been her third confessor and chief director, and was then minister-general of the Dominicans, began his admirable history of her. This was finished in 1395. Raimondo's Latin text was first published in 1553 in Cologne. An Italian version, begun by one of the Saint's secretaries, Neri di Landoccio Pagliaresi, was printed at the Dominican convent of San Jacopo di Ripoli near Florence, in 1477. Another edition, which differs considerably, was printed at Milan in 1489. Instead, however, of all of these, a comparatively modern Italian translation by the Canonico Bernardino Pecci, first published by Girolamo Gigli at Siena in 1707, surpasses them all."

177

**The Beginning
of Catherine's Canonization**

*Gardner writes in the original preface to
his biography of St. Catherine: "Second
in date and in importance [among the
textual evidences for her life] to the
Legenda comes the* Processus. *At the
time it was compiled, she had not yet
been canonized by the Church, even
though the feast of 'a certain person
called and named the blessed Catherine
of Siena' was being annually celebrated in the Dominican convents and
churches of Venice and elsewhere, and
pictures of her were being painted for
veneration in many places. This led
to some complaints. So the* Processus,
*Latin for 'process,' was commissioned in
order to establish her sainthood through
evidence. It is a collection of testimonies
and letters by Catherine's surviving followers and others who had come under
her influence, edited (so to speak) by Fra
Tommaso Caffarini between 1411–13,
with a few later additions."*

great wonder and consolation of all, she rose from her couch unaided and received the blessed sacrament from his hands. Afterward, she relapsed into her motionless condition, but had recovered her speech sufficiently to talk freely with Bartolomeo during the few days that he remained in Rome.

After a while, Bartolomeo's duty called him back to Siena, and she gave him her last command that he should make himself the constant companion of Fra Raimondo, who would soon be elected minister-general of the Dominican Order. The friar then implored her for a sign that she would regain her health before he had to go. Accordingly, on the following day he found her merry and joyful; she stretched out her arms and tenderly embraced him before he left for Siena. Raimondo's account is recorded in the *Processus:* "But if I may speak with the words of the prophet, I was 'seduced by the Lord' [see Jer. 20:7], and decided to set out. But after I reached my convent in Siena I was informed by a letter from one of her sons that, on that very day, not long after my departure, she had returned to the same state of inability to move her body, just as before. Then, after a few days, as the *Legenda* recounts, she blissfully passed from this dying life and valley of tears to the long-desired and sweet embraces of her bridegroom."

A few days after Bartolomeo left, Stefano Maconi finally arrived in Rome. Catherine's last letter to him playfully bids him to come, or else she will get him no more indulgences. And while she gives no hint to him of her own approaching death, she also seems surprised, perhaps a little hurt, when mentioning a report that Stefano intends to become a monk (of which he had told her nothing). It was his place to write what seems to have been the last letter of Catherine of Siena: "Write, my son Stefano," she said, "to Siena to Fra Bartolomeo and tell him that the Lord is exercising his mercy upon me and therefore let him, and all his companions in San Domenico, beg Jesus to allow me to offer up my life, even to the shedding of my blood for his glory, in order to illuminate the face of the Church."

The end came after prolonged suffering on April 29, the Sunday before the Ascension. A few hours before dawn, all the spiritual family were summoned, and Giovanni Tantucci gave her the absolution, *a culpa et a poena,* an indulgence granted by the pope at the hour of death. When day came, extreme unction was administered by the abbot of Sant'Antimo.

Catherine lay as though she were unconscious, but shortly after receiving the unction she began to move her face and arms

A Priestly Indulgence

As Gardner recounts, this popular indulgence was given to Catherine of Siena on her deathbed: a culpa et a poena. This was a popular phrase throughout the later Middle Ages, and means that the sinner is freed from both the penalty (poena) of sins against God and neighbor, and also from the guilt (culpa) of those sins. In Catherine's day, this indulgence, or remission, was granted only to those who expressed sincere contrition—unlike the way indulgences often functioned in the centuries of the Renaissance, where they could be purchased at will.

A Novelist Imagines
the Deathbed Scene

"On Sunday, the twenty-ninth of April, shortly before dawn, Alessia and Mona Lapa saw that the end was near. Catherine's breathing was becoming stertorous. Everyone in the house assembled. Master Tantucci pronounced over her the plenary indulgence the Pope had granted her for the hour of death. Catherine promptly asked that the pronouncement should be repeated, for two popes had granted that indulgence to her, and once more her will prevailed. . . . Suddenly she showed signs of an inner struggle, raising her arms, as if to ward off blows. . . . Then her expression became calm and serene again. 'Stefano . . .' 'Mamma . . . oh, mamma . . .' 'I want you to join the Carthusian Order, Stefano.' 'I will join it, mamma.' 'Give Neri my love . . . give my love . . . to all . . . my children.' Her voice sank to a murmur, and from then on only God could hear her. Outside, the sun was rising."

(De Wohl, 358)

as though enduring a last assault from evil spirits. This lasted nearly two hours. Again and again, she said: *"Peccavi, Domine, miserere mei"* [an allusion to Ps. 51:1, 4, meaning "I have sinned against God; have mercy"] and *"Credo, credo"* ["I believe; faith"]. And once, after having been silent for a while, she said with a joyous countenance, as if in response to an accusation she had just heard: "Never vainglory, but always the true glory and praise of Jesus Christ crucified."

Then they helped her to sit up, and she began making a general confession. "She spoke," writes Barduccio, "like one who was starving for the blood of Christ." Turning to those of her spiritual children who were not present at her last will and testament several days earlier, she now told each of them what she would have him or her do after her death. Pointing to Stefano with her finger she said, "And you, I command in the name of God to go to the Carthusian Order, for God has called and chosen you for that." Let Barduccio tell the rest: "Making the sign of the cross, she blessed us all, and then she approached her desired end, persevering in prayer and saying, 'Lord, you summon me to yourself, and I am coming, not by my own merits, but solely through your mercy, which I crave from you in virtue of your blood.' And at last, she cried out many times: *Sangue, Sangue* [Italian for "blood"]. Finally, after the example of our Savior, she said, 'Father, into your hands I commend my soul and my spirit,' and sweetly, with her face like an angel's, she bowed down her head and gave up the ghost."

Stefano carried the body to the church of the Minerva, where it lay until the evening of Tuesday, May 1, exposed to the veneration of the people. Pope Urban himself had the funeral carried out with all ecclesiastical pomp, and Giovanni Cenci, the senator of Rome, had another requiem offered in the name of the Roman people. Thus, for one brief moment, the papacy and the Republic of Rome seem to have met in harmony and union by the side of Catherine's tomb.

CHAPTER FIFTEEN
Her Literary Legacy

As we saw in the last chapter, in her second letter to Fra
Raimondo Catherine thought of the written legacy she would
leave behind at the end of her life. We saw her commend her
works to her spiritual son. The *literary* value of these remains
is probably the last thing that the saint would have concerned
herself with; she was not, in any normal sense of the words,
a "woman of letters." Nevertheless, her spiritual and mystical
writings rank among the classics of the Italian language, and
hold a position of unique importance in the literature of the
fourteenth century.

The importance of the *Dialogue* in the history of Italian literature has never been fully realized. In a language that is singularly
poor in mystical works (although rich in almost every other field
of thought), it stands with the *Divine Comedy* as one of the two
supreme attempts to express the eternal in the symposium of a
day, to paint the union of the soul with the suprasensible while
still imprisoned in the flesh. The whole of Catherine's life is the
realization of the end of Dante's poem: "to remove those living
in this life from a state of misery, and to lead them to the state of
faithfulness." And the mysticism of Catherine's book is as practical and altruistic as that of Dante's, as when he declares to his
patron, Cangrande della Scala, that the whole *Divine Comedy* "was
undertaken for work, not for speculation." Thus Catherine, in
the preliminary chapters of the *Dialogue* makes her first petition
to the eternal Father for herself only because "the soul cannot
perform any true service to her neighbor by teaching, example,
or prayer, unless she first services herself by acquiring virtue."

Letter from St. Catherine to Stefano Maconi

The resemblance at times between Catherine's phraseology and thought with that of Dante, in the *Dialogue* and in the letters, is not entirely coincidental. Although she never mentions the poet, and assuredly had never read the *Divine Comedy*, she must have frequently heard lines quoted by her followers. Neri di Landoccio, at least, appears to have been a Dante student. We might imagine those passages that were read aloud in Catherine's circle: the mystical espousals of St. Francis with Poverty, the praises of St. Dominic, or St. Bernard's invocation to the Blessed Virgin; and saint and secretaries alike were probably fired by the music of him who had fought the same battle for righteousness more than half a century before.

The end of one of Catherine's longest letters to Fra Raimondo reads almost like a first sketch of the *Dialogue,* and contains the vision that was to be the starting point of that book. Catherine claims to have learned to write by a miracle, the power having suddenly come to her by a kind of spiritual intuition while staying at the Rocca d'Orcia in the autumn of 1377. "This letter," she says, "and another that I sent you, I have written with my own hand on the Isola della Rocca, with many sighs and an abundance of tears, so that the eye, though seeing, saw not. I was full of wonder at myself and at the goodness of God, considering his mercy towards the creatures that possess reason—and his providence, that so abounded towards me so that, for my refreshment, he gave me and prepared me to receive the faculty of writing so that I might have somewhere to relieve my heart. In a wonderful way, God set my mind to be able to do this, as the master does to the child when he shows him how to copy. As soon as you had left me, with the glorious evangelist John and Thomas of Aquinas, I began to learn in my sleep. Forgive me for writing too much, for my hands and my tongue are in tune with my heart."

Catherine stands with Petrarch as the second greatest letter writer of the fourteenth century. It is interesting that, although the dates of their correspondence overlap (the saint probably began writing letters in 1370, the year she entered public life, although the majority of those that have been preserved date from 1376–79), and they were to some extent battling in the same cause, they had only three correspondents in common: Charles V of France; Francesco di Bartolomeo Casini, a physician; and Bonaventura Badoara, the cardinal of Padua. In Petrarch's letters to Pope Urban V we find something of the same spirit that inspired Catherine in writing to Popes Gregory XI and Urban VI. But as a rule, their epistolary styles are poles apart; Catherine's language is the purest Tuscan of the golden age of the Italian vernacular, far removed from Petrarch's would-be Ciceronian Latin. The simple but profound philosophy underlying all of Catherine's writings is the same that, put into practice, armed her to pass unsubdued and unshaken through the great game of the world.

In addition to the book and the letters, twenty-six prayers have been preserved that Catherine uttered on various occasions. The shortest one is said to be the first thing she ever wrote with her own hand:

> O holy Spirit, come into my heart. By Thy power draw it to Thee, its God, and grant me love with fear. Guard me, Christ, from every evil thought. Warm me and enflame me with Thy most sweet love, so that every pain may seem light to me. My holy Father and my sweet Master, help me now in all my ministry. Christ Love, Christ Love, Amen.

The others are mystical outpourings that were taken down at the time by the saint's disciples, and repeat in similar and slightly varied forms the aspirations that breathe from her other writings.

CHAPTER SIXTEEN
Dissolution of the Fellowship

The spirit of St. Catherine did not live on by written words alone after her death. She also left behind a devoted company of men and women, trained by her in the cell of self-knowledge, pledged to consecrate their lives to righteousness, to labor for the unity and reformation of the church.

With her last breath, Catherine deputed Monna Alessa to succeed her as head of the *famiglia*, while all in general were to look to Fra Raimondo for spiritual direction. William Flete and Messer Matteo Cenni were to preside over the continuation of her work in Siena itself. However, even though the correspondence shows that they all kept closely associated for years, the actual fellowship inevitably broke up, each one going the way that Catherine had pointed out to him. Alessa herself didn't survive much longer than her beloved friend, and died shortly afterward in Rome.

Fra Raimondo was in Genoa when Catherine died, preparing to go by sea to Pisa on the way to Bologna, where a general chapter meeting of the Dominicans loyal to Urban was about to be held. The friar tells us that he was full of apprehension, both because of the storm that was raging at sea and because he feared the Clementines (the opposing faction of the Dominicans at that time) were lying in wait for him. At Bologna, he was elected master-general, in opposition to the leader of the Clementines, and the schism in the Dominican Order was complete.

Raimondo's task as master-general was one that would have even tried the powers of a much stronger man. He found the whole order rent by the schism, with individual convents being

187

either practically deserted or else corrupt and rebellious. The most he could do was to decree that in every province under his obedience there should be at least one convent of the regular observance, containing at least twelve friars, in which the original rule of St. Dominic should be maintained in all its pristine severity. Meanwhile, at the general chapter of the Clementine obedience held at Avignon in 1386, Raimondo and his fellow friars were denounced and threatened with punishment under the constitutions of the order.

Even the friars of the Roman obedience murmured against the reform, and in 1395, Raimondo issued an encyclical letter denying that he was dividing the order and disorganizing convents. At the same time, Raimondo was worn out by illness and distracted by the political missions undertaken on behalf of Pope Urban and his successor, in Sicily and elsewhere. He was of too gentle a nature to adopt severe measures.

In 1396, Raimondo went to Germany to urge on the work of reform there, and he never returned. He died in Nuremberg on October 5, 1399, leaving a memory of charity and personal holiness. But the Acts of the chapter held in that city in 1405, under his successor, Tommaso da Fermo, show clearly that Raimondo's work as a reformer had been ineffectual. And after the schism ended some years later, Fra Leonardo da Firenze painted a deplorable picture of the general corruption of the Dominican Order in 1421.

It is only left to mention a few other of Catherine's closest friends. The great friendship that bound Neri di Landoccio to Stefano Maconi remained unbroken until the former's death. In obedience to Catherine's dying instructions, and despite the opposition of his family, Stefano joined the Carthusians in the spring of 1381. "I tell you, dearest brother," he wrote on May 30 to Neri, "our benign God in his goodness and not because of my merits has turned his mercy towards me, a wretched man, and has allowed me to receive the holy habit. I write this to you so that you may partake with me of the sweet joy and gladness that my soul feels. I won't tell you everything that led to this coming to pass . . . but I will at least tell you this: our holy Mamma showed and promised this to me, so emphatically, at her blessed end." In the following year, to his great disappointment, he was made prior of Pontignano. He wrote again to Neri, "My sweet brother, I ask you to have compassion on me and aid me with holy prayer, asking God to give me grace to correct my life and be his true servant even to the end, and that he may grant me to bear the weight that he has deigned to lay upon my shoulders." In 1389, Stefano was transferred to Milan and made prior of the Carthusian convent of Our Lady of St. Ambrose. There he was influential in keeping the Milanese despot faithful and obedient to Pope Urban, and in furthering the interests of the Commune of Siena at his court. By 1398, Stefano was elected prior-general of the whole Carthusian Order under the Roman obedience, in opposition to the Carthusians who were adhering to the popes of Avignon. A letter written to Fra Tommaso survives in which Stefano informs him of the election, asks for his prayer and for those of Fra Raimondo, and, now that he will no longer reside inside Italy, commits the book of Catherine's letters and her other relics to Tommaso's care.

"It is pleasant to imagine that we might see idealized portraits of Stefano and Bartolommeo among the white-robed Carthusians who are bearing their crosses after Christ in Ambrogio Borgognone's painting."

Neri di Landoccio, mean-while, had fulfilled Catherine's wish by becoming a hermit, first near Florence, and then, near Siena. He kept in close touch with the surviving members of the fellowship, gathered disci-ples around him, and lived a life of austere holiness. He died on March 12, 1406, and was buried at the convent of the Olivetani outside Porta Tufi.

Catherine's other secretary, Francesco Malavolti, remained in the world for several years after her death. After his wife and children died, an uncle advised him to become a knight of St. John, rather than marry again. Francesco resolved to do this and was accepted by the

Neri di Landoccio

Vida Scudder offers some additional sug-gestions as to Neri's role in Catherine's famiglia, in the years after her death: "In the precious collection of letters by St. Catherine's disciples . . . the greater number are addressed to Neri. We gain from them the impression that after her death, as before, he was the center of the little group. We have charming touches concerning his pursuits, as when Giunta di Grazia writes him from Naples concerning a borrowed volume of Dante, or Stefano thanks him for a copy of original verses, and tells how he has had them choicely illumined and given them away. For Neri was a poet of some excellence—author of graceful lauds in praise of Catherine, and of a rhymed Saint-legend. He also prob-ably translated into Italian, at least in part, the Latin Legenda of his blessed mother, written by Fra Raimondo of Capua" (Scudder 2, ix–x).

chapter-general of the order at Genoa and returned to Siena to prepare the armor, weapons, and horse that he needed. But in the night before the day on which he was to be knighted, Catherine appeared to him in a vision, rebuking him for still clinging to the vanities of the world, and asked him to rise, seek out Neri, and go with him to the convent of Monte Oliveto Maggiore, where he would be received without opposition. The next day, Francesco sold the armor, weapons, and horse, and distributed the proceeds to the poor, receiving the habit on the same evening, the vigil of St. Lucy in 1388.

191

**Catherine Spared
the Ultimate Disappointment?**

*After Catherine's death, the papacy
spiraled further down into despair
and disrepair, and her spiritual father,
Pope Urban VI, finally fell. "She was
spared the sight of Urban's fall, and
was not doomed to witness the shame,
the blood and the madness in which 'her
most sweet Christ on earth' ended his
unhappy pontificate" (Gardner, 65).*

This brings us to Urban. With Catherine's death, all thoughts of reformation seem to have died out of the pope's heart, and he began to tread the path on which the popes of the Renaissance were to follow. He had already formally deprived Queen Giovanna of her kingdom and all her fiefs, releasing her subjects from their allegiance to her or else face excommunication. This happened in April 1380. To defend herself from him and her Hungarian cousins, Giovanna adopted Louis of Anjou as her heir and appealed to Clement and the French for protection. In the autumn, Charles of Durazzo entered Italy with a Hungarian army and, at the beginning of June 1381, was crowned in Rome by Urban as king of Naples and Jerusalem, under the title of Charles III. We are not concerned with the ensuing struggle between Charles and Louis, or with the miserable deaths of both competitors—Louis dying of the plague at Bari in 1384, and Charles by the hands of assassins in Visegrad in 1386. In the previous year, Charles had broken with Urban, had been solemnly excommunicated by him, and had sent his army to besiege him in Nocera. It was on this occasion that Urban committed one of the most appalling crimes of the age. At Nocera in January 1385, just before the siege, he discovered what was probably nothing more than a design on the part of certain members of the curia to restrain him for the good of the church, but which his suspicious mind magnified into a plot against his life. The bishop of Aquila and six cardinals, including the English Benedictine Adam Easton, were promptly arrested and subjected to prolonged tortures. While Urban himself walked in the garden reading his breviary aloud, plugging his ears to their cries, a pirate of Genoese origin was appointed to do the torturing. When he was finally released from Nocera, after the siege, by the remnant of the army of Louis of Anjou, Urban dragged his prisoners with him. He had the bishop of Aquila, who was too maimed to walk, butchered along the way. Adam Easton he set free through the intervention of Richard II. The other five he took with him to Genoa in September and imprisoned them in his house. None of these unfortunate men were ever seen again. When Pope Urban left Genoa in December 1386, they were either thrown into the sea or strangled and buried in quicklime under the stables of the house. The rest of the Sacred College shrank from Urban in horror, except for a few insignificant Neapolitans whom he had recently made into bishops.

The tragedy of Urban's pontificate ended with his death in the Vatican on October 15, 1389. He who had set out as a strenuous reformer of the church and a friend of the servants of God, ended his days in the worst corruption and bloodshed, his authority denied even the Italian powers that had acknowledged him as pope.

After Urban, and a Schism Eventually Ends

Ignoring the claims of the rival College of Cardinals at Avignon, fourteen cardinals in Rome elected a successor to Urban VI on November 2: the cardinal of Naples, Pietro Tomacelli, a prudent and virtuous man. He took the name Boniface IX. Five years later, Clement VII died in Avignon, and Pedro de Luna was elected his successor, taking the title of Benedict XIII. Always gracious and magnanimous, never yielding to excess anger or

193

vindictiveness, to all appearances he remained as devout a man as when he had attracted the sympathy of St. Catherine. Benedict XIII remained determined to maintain the papacy of Avignon. On the other side, Boniface IX began to restore the temporal power of the papacy in Rome, by destroying the freedoms of the Roman Republic in 1398, rebuilding Castelle Sant'Angelo as a fortress to overawe the city, and crushing the count of Fondi, whose fiefs had embedded themselves in the papal states.

As prior-general of the Carthusians of the Roman obedience, Stefano Maconi worked zealously to bring the schism to an end. He started first with his own order. In 1402, he wrote a long letter to the fathers of the Grand Chartreuse, urging them to be one body and spirit, offering to lay down his own office for the sake of unity. He told again the story of his angelic mother, Catherine, and the letter that Stefano himself had written to them, at her dictation, when she first heard that they were about to follow the party of the schismatics. "Come, then, to our common mother, my brothers," Stefano wrote. "Fulfill my joy, for I have nothing more at heart than your salvation, to serve the divine glory together with you, and to behold the unity of the Christian republic under its lawful head and ruler, the Roman pontiff."

The younger monks were moved by Stefano's letter, and probably would have answered in kind, if it wasn't for the strenuous opposition of their old leader, Dom Guillaume. But in June of that year, Dom Guillaume died and was succeeded as prior-general of the order under the obedience of Benedict XIII by Boniface Ferrer. Stefano didn't have to wait long, then, for a favorable reply to his appeal.

After Boniface IX, in Rome, came the short and stormy pontificate of Innocent VII. Then came the election of Angelo

Correr, who was then the patriarch of Constantinople, and who had been closely associated with Catherine's surviving followers in Venice. Angelo took the title of Pope Gregory XII. At once, Gregory XII expressed his wish to meet and confer with Benedict XIII, declaring that he would go in a fishing boat, if no real galley was available, or on foot with his staff, if he couldn't get a horse. And Benedict, on his part, expressed a similar eagerness for the two to meet.

Thus, two men, two popes, faced each other who had both received Catherine's words while she was alive. In each of them, Catherine had seen a possible reformer of the church. But after many negotiations, with each claimant desiring for the meeting to take place in a city subject to his own obedience, high hopes all began to once again fall apart. The patience of the Catholic world was now exhausted. In May 1408, France withdrew her allegiance from Benedict, who fled to Perpignan; and the cardinals of the Roman obedience met those that had deserted Benedict, and the united sacred colleges summoned the bishops of Christendom to a council.

The council met in Pisa on March 25, 1409. Only two of the princes of the church who had shared in the conclave that elected Urban, and knew how the Schism had happened, were still alive: Benedict himself, and the aged cardinal of Poitiers, Guy de Malesset, who now presided over the deliberations of the assembly. On June 5, the council deposed both Gregory and Benedict as heretics and schismatics. The *Te Deum* rose up from the cathedral of Pisa to thank God for the deliverance of his church; the bells rang out, and were caught up by the campanili of village after village, until the news reached Florence. On June 26, twenty-four cardinals—fourteen who had previously acknowledged Gregory, and ten, for Benedict—elected the

St. Catherine's Stigmata

Gardner barely mentions what is one of the famous aspects of St. Catherine's life in the tradition of Catholic piety: the gift of the stigmata in her body. Gardner alludes to the event in his opening to chapter 5, and then briefly tells the story of how it happened in Pisa, in chapter 7, before alluding to it once again here. St. Francis of Assisi was the first person to be graced with these sufferings, and Catherine made claim to the same, although, at her request, God made the wounds invisible until just after her death, when they were visible to those gathered around her.

There was great disagreement about Catherine's claims, even in her own day, and in the century following. These disagreements were not without political overtones; the Franciscans had had exclusive claims to this wonder up until the claims of Catherine, a Dominican. And the Franciscan Pope Sixtus IV decreed, a century after Catherine, that the stigmata belonged to St. Francis alone. The opinion of most Catholics has changed since then, and Catherine of Siena is almost always recognized as the first woman to be granted this special way of suffering with Christ.

It is not surprising that our biographer gives relatively little attention to St. Catherine's stigmata, as Gardner was in many ways a child of the modernist era of religious biography, inaugurated by the French scholar, Ernest Renan, and his ways of providing natural

cardinal archbishop of Milan, Peter Philargis, a Franciscan of Greek origin, who assumed the title of Pope Alexander V.

It is uncertain whether or not Stefano Maconi was actually present at the council, but it is quite clear that, despite his personal friendship with Gregory, he now declared unhesitatingly for Pope Alexander V. He had already written again to the fathers of the Grande Chartreuse declaring that the council of Pisa was lawful and canonical, that the cardinals were inspired by the Holy Ghost, and whomever they elected pope would undoubtedly be the true vicar of Christ.

The prolonged struggle in which St. Catherine and he had borne so much was now concluded, and Stefano's one desire was to be free to give himself entirely to divine contemplation. By 1421, "after his earnest entreaties, because of his old age, his infirmities, and the many labors undertaken for the order," Stefano was allowed to resign his office of prior of the Certosa of Pavia. In spite of invitations from elsewhere, he chose to remain in the Certosa of Pavia and it was there, on August 7, 1424, that he passed away, with the names of Mary and Catherine on his lips.

explanations for the miraculous, in the lives of Jesus or the saints. Gardner's mention of Catherine's stigmata on this last page of his biography is careful not to deny the truth of it, but to minimize its importance in the life of the saint.

When Tommaso Caffarini died in 1434, the last of Catherine's spiritual family had joined her again. But already, the movement she started had come to an end, to be renewed half a century later in another form and without success, by Fra Girolamo Savonarola (1452–98) on the one hand, and on the other, by the mystical sacrifice of several famous women, clad in the habit she had worn and bearing the same marks of Christ's passion on their bodies: Lucia of Narni (1476–1544), Osanna of Mantua (1449–1505), and Colomba of Rieti (1467–1501). These Dominican tertiaries attempted to imitate St. Catherine's work among the corrupt courts of the Renaissance.

Ostensibly, Catherine's labor had failed. A century after her death, the state of her beloved Italy was more deplorable than when she had departed from it. The papacy was immeasurably more corrupt than it had been even during the time of the Great Schism, and far greater divisions were about to appear in the church. But the true value of the work to which the whole power of a human soul has been dedicated—and certainly that of a small religious movement—cannot be measured only by its outward and visible effects. Its most perfect flowers and fruits throughout the ages are in the invisible garden of the spirit, grown to be gathered only by the One who feeds among the lilies.

ACKNOWLEDGMENTS

All quotations from the Holy Bible are taken from the translation of the New Jerusalem Bible, used by permission. The quote from St. John of the Cross that begins the sixth chapter is from the translation of E. Allison Peers, translator and editor, *The Complete Works of St. John of the Cross*, vol. 2, 3rd rev. ed. (Westminster, MD: Newman Press, 1953), page 418. At those frequent occasions when Gardner quotes from the writings of Fra Raimondo, prefacing the quote with "Fra Raimondo writes," or something similar, he is always quoting from his own translation of the Latin *Legenda*. These translations have been updated into contemporary English for the present edition of Gardner's biography; they have also sometimes been condensed, with or without the use of ellipses. Among other quotations from the words of St. Catherine, most are from Catherine's letters, and the principles followed have been the same as for quotes from the *Legenda*.

BIBLIOGRAPHY

The following sources are referenced in the sidebar notes.

BELL: Rudolph M. Bell, *Holy Anorexia*. Chicago: University of Chicago Press, 1987.

BONAVENTURE: St. Bonaventure, *Life of Saint Francis*. Translation mine.

BRIDGET: St. Bridget of Sweden, "Extracts from the *Liber Celestis.*" In *Medieval Writings on Female Spirituality*, edited by Elizabeth Spearing. New York: Penguin Books, 2002.

BYNUM: Caroline Walker Bynum, *Holy Feast and Holy Fast: The Religious Significance of Food to Medieval Women*. Berkeley: University of California Press, 1987.

CAVALLINI: Giuliana Cavallini, OP, *Catherine of Siena*. New York: Continuum, 2005.

CRUM: Roger J. Crum and John T. Paoletti, eds., *Renaissance Florence: A Social History*. Cambridge, UK: Cambridge University Press, 2006.

DE WOHL: Louis De Wohl, *Lay Siege to Heaven: A Novel about Saint Catherine of Siena*. Fort Collins, CO: Ignatius Press, 1991.

DRANE: Augusta Theodosia Drane, *The History of St. Catherine of Siena and Her Companions*, 3rd ed., 2 vols. New York: Longmans, Green & Co., 1899.

FERRETTI: Lodovico Ferretti, *Saint Catherine of Siena*. Siena, It.: Edizioni Cantagalli, 1996.

GARDNER: Edmund G. Gardner, *The Story of Siena and San Gimignano*. London: J. M. Dent & Co., 1905.

JORGENSEN: Johannes Jorgensen, *Saint Bridget of Sweden*, vols. 1–2, trans. Ingeborg Lund. New York: Longmans, Green, and Co., 1954.

MEISS: Millard Meiss, *Painting in Florence and Siena After the Black Death: The Arts, Religion and Society in the Mid-Fourteenth Century*. New York: Harper & Row, 1973.

MISCIATTELLI: Piero Misciattelli, *The Mystics of Siena*, trans. M. Peters-Roberts. New York: D. Appleton and Company, 1930.

O'DRISCOLL: Mary O'Driscoll, *Catherine of Siena: Passion for the Truth, Compassion for Humanity*. Hyde Park, NY: New City Press, 2005.

SABATIER: Paul Sabatier, *The Road to Assisi: The Essential Biography of St. Francis*, ed. Jon M. Sweeney. Orleans, MA: Paraclete Press, 2004.

SCUDDER 1: Vida D. Scudder, trans. and ed., *Saint Catherine of Siena As Seen in Her Letters*. New York: E. P. Dutton & Co., 1905.

SCUDDER 2: Vida D. Scudder, *The Disciple of a Saint: Being the Imaginary Biography of Raniero di Landoccio dei Pagliaresi*. New York: E. P. Dutton & Co., 1907.

INDEX OF NAMES AND SUBJECTS

About Paraclete Press

WHO WE ARE

PARACLETE PRESS is a publisher of books, recordings, and DVDs on Christian spirituality. Our publishing represents a full expression of Christian belief and practice—from Catholic to Evangelical, from Protestant to Orthodox.

We are the publishing arm of the Community of Jesus, an ecumenical monastic community in the Benedictine tradition. As such, we are uniquely positioned in the marketplace without connection to a large corporation and with informal relationships to many branches and denominations of faith.

WHAT WE ARE DOING

BOOKS | Paraclete publishes books that show the richness and depth of what it means to be Christian. Although Benedictine spirituality is at the heart of all that we do, we publish books that reflect the Christian experience across many cultures, time periods, and houses of worship. We publish books that nourish the vibrant life of the church and its people—books about spiritual practice, formation, history, ideas, and customs.

We have several different series, including the best-selling Living Library, Paraclete Essentials, and Paraclete Giants series of classic texts in contemporary English; A Voice from the Monastery—men and women monastics writing about living a spiritual life today; award-winning literary faith fiction and poetry; and the Active Prayer Series that brings creativity and liveliness to any life of prayer.

RECORDINGS | From Gregorian chant to contemporary American choral works, our music recordings celebrate sacred choral music through the centuries. Paraclete distributes the recordings of the internationally acclaimed choir Gloriæ Dei Cantores, praised for their "rapt and fathomless spiritual intensity" by *American Record Guide*, and the Gloriæ Dei Cantores Schola, which specializes in the study and performance of Gregorian chant. Paraclete is also the exclusive North American distributor of the recordings of the Monastic Choir of St. Peter's Abbey in Solesmes, France, long considered to be a leading authority on Gregorian chant.

DVDS | Our DVDs offer spiritual help, healing, and biblical guidance for life issues: grief and loss, marriage, forgiveness, anger management, facing death, and spiritual formation.

Learn more about us at our Web site:
www.paracletepress.com, or call us toll-free at 1-800-451-5006.

You may also be interested in . . .

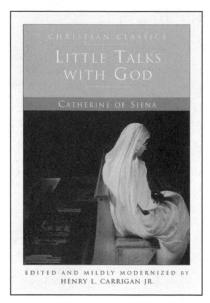

Little Talks with God
Catherine of Siena
ISBN: 978-1-55725-272-2
$14.95, Paperback

In this intense and searching work, Catherine offers up petitions to God, filling her conversation with instruction on discernment, true and false spiritual emotion, obedience, and truth, and revealing her famous image of Christ as the Bridge.

The Road to Assisi: The Essential Biography of St. Francis
Edited by Jon M. Sweeney
ISBN: 978-1-55725-401-6
$14.95, Paperback

He conversed with both the pope and the sultan. He transformed a taste for fine things and trouba-dour poetry into greater loves for poverty and joyful devotion to God. He never intended to found a traditional religious "movement," but nevertheless, he did. This foundational biography explores who Francis of Assisi was, and what we can learn from his life.

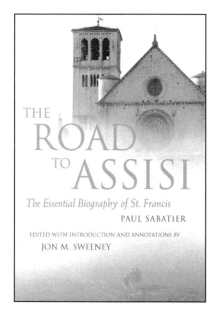